Job Search Strategies:

Get A Good Job Even in a Bad Economy

A Professional Career Coach Shares Strategies that Work

My name is Bud Clarkson and I work as a career consultant in the outplacement industry. During the past few years I have walked nearly 500 people through the career transition process. I've learned real-world strategies for successful job search from them and from the more than 100 other career consultants with whom I network regularly.

Job Search Strategies: Get a Good Job Even in a Bad Economy is designed to shorten your job search, increase your confidence and provide the inside information you need to understand how companies in today's market make hiring decisions... and therefore, what you have to do to land the good job you deserve.

Bud Clarkson

Job Search Strategies:

Get A Good Job Even in a Bad Economy

A Professional Career Coach Shares Strategies That Work

Bud Clarkson

Contents

Foreword

The New York Times reported on January 9, 2009 that the number of unemployed persons in the United States was 11.1 million. However, the Bureau of Labor Statistics does not count the following persons as unemployed:

- Persons who lost a job, found a part-time job, but are still looking for a full-time job

- Persons who lost a job, looked for a job, didn't find one and gave up looking *less* than a year ago

- Persons who lost a job, looked for a job, didn't find one and gave up looking *more* than a year ago

The fact is that the government's official unemployment rate does not count the millions of Americans who were unable to find a job or were unable to find full-time employment.[i] Reality is that there are millions of Americans who are unemployed, underemployed or discouraged and not even trying to find a job.

Are you in one of those categories? This book is for you!

It is especially for you if you don't have the benefit of outplacement services. If you're not familiar with the term, it refers to the business of helping displaced workers find new employment. People who deliver those services are usually called career coaches or career consultants. There are also thousands of independent career coaches, many of whom are reputable and skilled; some of whom are not.

I work as a career consultant in the outplacement industry and over the past few years have walked 500 people through the career transition process. I've learned real-world strategies for successful job searches from them and from the more than 100 other career consultants in my professional network.

The purpose of this book is to share those valuable lessons with you in an easy-to-read format.

This is simple but powerful information that will shorten your job search, increase your confidence and provide the inside information you need to understand how companies in today's market make hiring decisions... and therefore, what you have to do to land a job.

In each chapter you will read about one critical aspect of the modern job search. I will tell you why the topic is important and explain clearly what you need to do about it. Many chapters include lists of job search strategies. These lists will help you find new ideas and new inspiration to structure your job search around strategies that get results.

I've been through career transition several times. I know from firsthand experience career transition can be emotionally draining and in worst cases, financially devastating. However, this book can help you avoid pitfalls and get you to your next job faster.

Yes, it's tough out there. However, there are jobs! I talk to people every day who have just landed a good job.

You can find work if you use the right strategies and persist. This book does not promise results without effort. However, the information in this book does provide a proven roadmap for results when mixed with perseverance and commitment.

Finally, I can tell you of one silver lining in the cloud of discouragement and anxiety you may be feeling right now. Many job search clients, once they land their next position, say this, "It was difficult... but it was a real opportunity to rethink my career and make some changes I had been thinking about for a long time."

So, here's to your success as you have this new opportunity to decide once more, "What do I want to be when I grow up?"

Anecdotes about my clients in this book are all accurate and real stories, but names and circumstances have been changed to protect privacy.

~The Author~

Introduction:
The New Job Search

This is not your daddy's job search. In fact, if your father is of a certain age, he probably never conducted more than one job search in his lifetime. He may have worked his entire career at the same company.

However, those days of one job or career for life are gone! Many say that the average worker today is likely to have five to seven jobs over the course of a career! (Actually, I don't know where they get those numbers. Who counts that kind of stuff?) Still, reality is that you will probably need the job search skills and strategies in this book more than once in your lifetime unless you are within a few years of retirement age right now – an age that keeps moving further into the future for most people!

The job search process has changed significantly in the recent past. Primary reasons include computerization and a growing use of the Internet. If you haven't done a job search in a while, you are going to find these trends:

- Online applications are everywhere

- Job postings have abandoned newspaper classified ads.

- Job postings have migrated to online job boards or to company websites.

- Job hunters and recruiters use professional networking websites such as www.linkedin.com.

- New social technologies and websites such as Twitter and Facebook are also being used as tools in the job search.

The old days of looking in the paper, finding an opening, sending in your résumé and answering a call to come in for an interview are gone!

New ways and new routes to job opportunities have taken over. If you are to succeed you absolutely must get ready to use them, which is the reason you have this book, of course! Your ability to adapt will help determine the answer to one of your big questions, "How long does it take to get a job these days?"

How Long Will It Take Me to Land My Next Job?

How long will it take you to land your next job? That depends on many factors:

1. Your industry
2. Your career field
3. Your work history
4. The national economy
5. The local economy
6. Your geographical location
7. Your readiness to relocate
8. The energy you invest in the job search
9. Your job search skills

Important Notice: you really only control the last two or three items! You may or may not be willing and able to relocate but even that decision may be complicated by consideration for others such as your spouse, parents or aged parents. However, you do control entirely the energy you invest in the job search and the level of job searching skill you develop.

That is why this book gives you tips for maintaining your motivation and focus and will provide the essential job search skills you need.

Your Job Skills Will NOT Get You a Job... But Your Job Search Skills Will

Kelly was employed by a major corporation for 20 years, starting at age 19 and working her way up to the position of brand manager. Her career was on a roll and she was due for another big promotion when, BANG! She was called in to a special meeting with Human Resources (HR) to find out that along with dozens of others, she had been laid off.

After a few days of dealing with the shock, she pulled herself together and began to aggressively job search. Several weeks later, she called me.

"Bud, I want some interview coaching!"

"OK," I replied, "what's the hurry? Got a big interview coming up?"

"No," she said, "but I want to be ready when I do because I know a bad interview can keep a person from getting a job."

"Tell me about that," I replied.

Kelly said, "My former boss told me how one of his outstanding employees applied for a transfer to another unit within our corporation. My boss supported the move and recommended him because he was an outstanding worker."

"Well, the employee went for an interview with the new hiring manager. Right after that, my boss got a call from the manager."

"He said to my boss, 'Why did you send that guy to me. His interview was horrible!'"

"My boss replied, 'Wait a minute. I know the guy. He is absolutely exceptional! His interviewing skills are the problem, not his job performance. Let me talk to him and call you back. Will you give him another chance?'"

"So the hiring manager agreed. My boss coached the employee about interviewing and sent him back. To make a long story short, he did well on his second interview and got the job."

"Wow," I said to Kelly, "that's quite a story."

"That's right," said Kelly, "and what I thought about was, 'What if the employee had been applying for a job outside the company instead of inside? My boss would never have gotten that phone call from the hiring manager and the employee would never have gotten a second chance. Even though his work skills were exceptional, he would have lost the opportunity because his interviewing skills were poor!"

That's exactly what you need to realize. Having job skills is not sufficient for landing a great job. You must have job search skills. This book can help you get them!

The Job Search Skills You Need

Here are some key job search skills you need:

- Managing time
- Planning your job search
- Setting goals for your job search activities
- Organizing a home office
- Researching companies
- Writing cover letters and résumés
- Networking and interacting socially with friends and strangers
- Using a computer for word processing and e-mails
- Searching the Internet

- Expressing yourself verbally in networking and interviewing

A Word about English as a Second Language

Many people live in America whose native tongue is not English. I have had natives of India or Mexico as clients on a number of occasions, for example. Some of them have spoken English flawlessly and with little accent.

However, if English is not your first language and your proficiency is not perfect, it just makes common sense to consider taking additional English as Second Language (ESL) classes as one part of your strategy for landing your next job.

If an interviewer has difficulty understanding you in an interview, it may very well cost you the opportunity!

Who Should Use This Book

Are you in one of the following categories?

- Currently unemployed or underemployed
- Hate your job and want to find a better one
- Your company does not provide outplacement services
- Aware that you need help navigating the job market

The information in this book will shorten your job search and help you find a better job. When you do find it, it will help you negotiate better compensation!

Also, based on my experience as a job search coach, there's at least one more group that needs this book: the vast number of unemployed people who are convinced they don't need any help with the job search!

Oh, I understand, you're very self-confident and after all it's just a matter of going on the Internet, finding some openings and sending in a well-written résumé. After that, you will be called in and dazzle 'em with your brilliance.

Right?

Wrong!

Sure, there's an off-hand chance it may happen like that, but in today's job market... probably not.

It's a little more complicated than that and you need the latest information and techniques if you are going to land the best possible job in the shortest amount of time.

What This Book Can Do For You

This book will make your job search easier, faster and more effective. It's packed with information you need to know presented in an easy-to-use format.

- New and necessary job search skills
- Trends in the modern job hunt
- Strategies for getting started
- Strategies for keeping yourself motivated
- Strategies for staying focused
- Surviving the job search blues
- Dealing with job search disappointment
- Strategies for dealing with stress
- What you need to do IMMEDIATELY after losing your job
- Strategies for organizing your home office
- Career planning strategies
- How to fill out an online application
- Strategies for improving your résumé

- How to create great cover letters
- Top job lead strategies
- Strategies for standing out from the crowd
- Strategies for locating job leads
- How to network effectively
- Common interview questions
- How to answer difficult interview questions
- The art of negotiating the best compensation possible

How to Use This Book

I don't really intend this book to be read through from beginning to end. It's a tool box. Pick the right tool for the job at hand.

You probably know a lot about job searching already. On the other hand, there may be a lot you don't know. After all, you don't search for a job that often. (Actually, if you search for a job often enough to be an expert in the job search – let's be honest – you probably have some kind of more serious issue going on… if you know what I mean.)

Anyway, the best way to use this book is skip around and get help for specific problems. The lists of strategies are there to give you some quick tips. Stuck in your job search? Just review the lists of strategies and try something you're not doing currently. It may be just the idea you need!

15 Strategies for Using This Book

Use this book if you need to…

1. Adjust your attitude and manage your emotions so you can get started, stay on track and keep your energy high.

2. Get organized so you can job search more efficiently and get better results in less time.

3. Plan your job search and use more effective methods that actually work in today's job market.

4. Learn how to use common job search tools in order to make your work easier and faster.

5. Learn ways to use a computer and the Internet to find job leads, make contacts and land a position.

6. Discover inside secrets of how companies hire and how to use that information to your advantage.

7. Create ways of presenting yourself that set you apart from the crowd and help you land the best job and compensation possible.

8. Write a résumé that will get interviews (or if you get someone else to write it, avoid being ripped off and evaluate the résumé your writer provided).

9. Find sources of job leads you may not have considered, including leads from the really huge hidden job market.

10. Effectively grow and utilize your personal and professional network for extra-ordinary job search results.

11. Knock the socks off your interviewers and make yourself an irresistible hiring choice.

12. Develop negotiating skills and techniques that will win a compensation package you never thought possible.

13. Plan to relocate across country to a better job market.

14. Continue your education and expand your earning potential.

15. Launch a completely new career for greater life satisfaction; perhaps even the fulfillment of a lifetime dream!

Seven Strategies and Resources for Developing the Job Search Skills You Need

Develop key job search skills you need using these strategies:

1. Use this book!

2. Hire a career coach.

3. Read online career transition blogs such as www.secretsofthejobhunt.com.

4. Use the job search organizing site www.jibberjobber.com.

5. Network with other people who are currently in career transition and pick their brains.

6. Take a basic computer course.

7. Join Toastmasters or take a speech course at a local community college.

Attitude is a little thing that makes a big difference.
~Winston Churchill~

1

Adopt the Right Attitude

In the movie 9-11 by Oliver Stone, two policemen lay trapped beneath the fallen wreckage of the twin towers. Pinned in place beneath a mountain of rubble, in fear of their lives, one of the cops begins to panic.

His partner says to him, "Get your head right!"

The panicked policeman snaps back to himself, finds a way to overcome his anxiety and somehow does find a way to get his head right.

The search for a job is not the equivalent of being crushed beneath two fallen skyscrapers, but the fact is your biggest hurdle in the job search will be to get your head right and keep your spirits up.

The right attitude can make a concrete difference in helping you land your next great opportunity. Your attitude affects the kind of emotional energy you produce and that is a core reason it is so critical to successful job searching.

Positive energy helps you make a positive impression on an interviewer or potential employer, and that is important. So get your head right!

Trust me - it's really important that you embrace the job search process.

I don't only mean you should start getting excited about your next job. I mean you should embrace the fact that locating and landing your next career opportunity will require much hard work!

As I have told hundreds of clients, "Searching for a job is a job." It's not an easy job and contrary to popular opinion, it is not strictly a desk job. If you want a great job in record time, you will have to get up and get out. Meeting people is a big part of the job search process, but we will talk more about that later.

The thing you need to know first of all is that job search requires effort and positive energy. You must use strategies to help keep your head right.

Surviving the Job Search Blues

Honestly, Marvin was difficult to deal with when I first started working with him as a career transition client. After 33 years with a major American corporation, he lost his job as part of a reduction in force. Sarcasm and criticism seeped out in almost everything he said.

As we worked together developing his résumé, I realized Marvin had been quite successful in his career and obviously had gotten along well with people. I wondered how that could be if he was as snarky and grumpy and hard to please with his colleagues as he was being with me.

Fortunately, I kept cool and consistently ignored his snippy little remarks as the first couple of weeks of our relationship went by. Then, it happened.

One day as I spoke with Marvin on the phone, his tone of voice seemed more subdued and quiet.

"What's up?" I asked Marvin.

He replied in a tone of voice that I can only describe as, well, humble!

He said, "Bud, I'm going to be honest with you. I don't know what's going on with me. I can't concentrate. It's like I'm walking around in a daze."

"Every day I push losing my job to the back of my mind and try not to think about it, but at the end of every day I have a killer tension headache."

"Bud," he asked, completely serious, "Is that normal? I hope it is."

Right then I realized something that should have been clear to me all along. Marvin was grieving the loss of his job.

"Marvin," I said, "What you are experiencing is grief. You've lost a job you had for 33 years."

What I said to myself was, "No wonder he's been acting like a jerk! He's angry, depressed and scared, all at the same time!"

Consider Marvin as you go through your own career transition. The fact of the matter is that career transition by definition causes grief because grief is the normal human reaction to any significant loss.

On top of the grief, there's stress - financial worries, pressures from a spouse, the feeling of potential rejection every time you send out a résumé, actual rejection every time you're turned down for a position and the loss of your normal and customary daily routines.

You need some strategies not to let this emotional roller coaster make you sick. Consider the following suggestions.

1. If you feel that you are going to harm yourself or others, please get professional help.

2. If you are developing dysfunctional coping habits such as drinking too much or overeating, recognize what you are doing and make a change to the positive habits listed.

3. Build a support network of people you can spill your guts to, including your spouse, minister, best friend, or a local pink slip networking group.

4. Increase your exercise routine and take the opportunity to get in shape. The endorphins will really help your mood!

5. Build your spiritual life. Get in touch with your source of strength. Pray, meditate and read literature that will produce positive thoughts.

6. Volunteer in order to get out and be around people. Do something that puts you in contact with someone who has bigger troubles than you do!

Dealing with Rejection

Rejection hurts. In fact, it can be a killer! That feeling of rejection will deplete all of your enthusiasm and energy if you dwell on it and let it get the best of you.

Many people tell me the hardest part of the job search process is dealing with the rejection! There's probably not too much anyone can say to make it easier. However, I once read three good suggestions:

1. Don't take the rejection personally.

2. Get feedback on why you were rejected.

3. Build a support network.[ii]

That third point may be the most important!

However, there's more you can do to deal with rejection.

Manage your expectations. Don't count your eggs before they hatch a job. Many people get an interview for a great position with a wonderful company and immediately stop all of their other job search activities. Don't be that person.

Stop thinking defeated thoughts. Watch your self-talk! "Oh, what's the use? I'm not really qualified for that job. They probably won't even consider me."

Know what? You're right! If you talk yourself out of applying, they won't consider you for the job – because they can't. You didn't apply! Hockey great Wayne Gretsky famously said, "You miss 100 percent of the shots you don't take." He was correct. You also won't be hired for 100 percent of the jobs for which you don't apply.

So on the one hand, don't get too excited. It's not over until the weight-challenged lady sings and makes a job offer. On the other hand, don't give up before you begin!

Finally, particularly guard yourself during the interview process. Many career consultants would advise you to learn all you can about the interviewing and hiring process used by any company considering you, the time-line involved, who the final decision maker is, where you are in that process and who else is being considered.

So many times interviewees just go along with the process and wait for an outcome and then are surprised or disappointed. Get feedback after each interview about how you did and how you stack up to the other candidates. The more you know about your competition the better.

Remember, even if the process gets down to only two candidates and you are one of them, you still only have a 50/50 chance. I know of many people who thought they were a shoo in because they were being flown around the country to be wined and dined by top executives, only to be turned down.

Assess the situation as realistically as you can. This will help keep your emotions steady and focused.

Here are some positive, yet realistic self-talk phrases to help you keep your head right if you are turned down.

- "Eventually the employer must choose. Being in the top two or three is disappointing, but it shows I am a very attractive candidate. It just didn't work out this time."

- "Some things are beyond my control, such as the hiring of an internal candidate. Another candidate may have had an advantage that I did not have."

- "When it comes down to the wire, there is only one chair to fill. I was not the only one turned down. I learned from this experience and that will make me even more competitive next time."

What Happened?... and Why You Need a Transition Statement

Much of our identity and perceived self-value is wrapped up in our jobs! It's amazing how embarrassing and painful it can be in the first weeks after being let go to be confronted with a simple question from a concerned neighbor such as, "What happened?"

By the way, it's not an American or male phenomena only. One of my candidates, a female native of India, felt completely humiliated by her job loss! She actually fell into a deep depression for a while.

Your reaction may not be that severe, but the point is, many people experience job loss not only as an inconvenience but also as keenly embarrassing.

So, here's a technique that will help you get off to a good start psychologically.

It is helpful to write down your transition statement, which is your stock answer to people when they find out that you are back in the job hunt and they want to know, "What happened?"

Words matter and the way you answer that kind of question is important, not so much to the person who asked, but to you!

Here are five things you need to know and do to write a transition statement:

- Your neighbors, friends and second cousins twice removed don't *really* care about the details of what happened; they're just curious.

- No matter how you *feel*, unless you were fired for cause, then the *fact* of the matter is that losing your job is not something to feel bad about. It just happened to you, as it has to millions of others.

- Networking is essential to a successful and speedy career transition. Every time you have opportunity to speak with someone about your job loss, that's good because then you can tell them what kind of job you are looking for next!

- Therefore you need a brief explanation that respects your own dignity, satisfies people's basic curiosity and informs them about your job needs.

- So you write down and practice saying your transition statement, which goes something like this:

Neighbor: "Hey, Joe, what's going on?"

You: "Hi, Jane. Well (put name of your company here) recently (downsized; made a reduction in force; has been going though hard times; whatever the circumstances may have been). Unfortunately, I was one of   (put number here) who lost their jobs. So, I am looking for (put type of position you want here) in the (put type of industry here) industry. Who do you know that could help me out with that?

Trust me on a couple of things. First, most people don't really want to know the gory details of who got chopped and who survived and why and why not and the unfairness of it all. Secondly, you may be surprised at how helpful people can be once you get over the embarrassment, let them know your situation in a matter-of-fact way and ask for their assistance.

Go ahead and write down your transition statement. Practice saying the words. Then get around people and let them know what's happened!

Dirty Tricks, Black Holes, White Lies and Pushy Spouses

Sure, the rejection feature of the job search is tough. In fact, for many, the *anticipation* of rejection, shame, embarrassment and humiliation are enough to paralyze. Overcome that and get a right attitude about your job search. Otherwise, you will find yourself too busy to search because of "important home projects".

Unfortunately, though, free-floating anxiety isn't the only discouragement bug floating around the job search environment. Here are a few other matters that can put your head in a nonproductive mind-set as well as some thoughts on how to cure yourself of these common job search ills.

I offer these thoughts in the vein of helping you expect the unexpected. An attitude of expecting the unexpected can help reduce the shock of a surprising turn of events and get you back on an emotional even keel faster.

Dirty Tricks and Black Holes

Evil HR professionals everywhere are conspiring to put every possible roadblock between you and your dream job.

OK, that's not true at all but sometimes it can feel that way!

Here are situations you may encounter that are going to feel completely unfair:

- **Personality profiles used for screening.** You are asked before applying to please go online and take a "personality test". So there you are looking at a computer screen, trying to figure out the correct answer to a question like, "Are you more like a cat or a dog?" (No, that's not a real question from a personality test but trust me, the actual questions are just as ambiguous.) Next week, you get a call, "We're sorry Mr. Jones, but the results of your personality assessment have disqualified you from further consideration." Oh, yes, it happens.

  So, what to do? Get over it. There are no cheat sheets. These tests are supposed to determine whether you would be a good fit for the company and job offered.

Adopt the attitude that you probably wouldn't want to work there anyway. Apparently, they aren't looking for intelligent, unique people like you. So just move on.

- **Stress interviews.** Yes, I know - all interviews have the potential to be stressful. However, a stress interview is a deliberate effort to rattle you during the interview. Naturally, this is not announced to you. For example, your interviewer may appear to be uninterested or even hostile. The interviewer may not make eye contact or sigh at your answers, interrupt you or ask demeaning questions. Why? Well of course, for the sadistic pleasure of the interviewers! Either that or the interviewers want to gauge how you may react to stressful situations.

  So, what to do? The obvious answer is stay calm and composed. Not so obvious: *how* do you stay calm and composed? After all, you don't *know* that this is a stress interview. Back to the obvious: either way, just remain calm.

- **Black holes.** One of the most common ways my clients set themselves up for frustration in the job search is by assuming that companies are as much in a hurry to hire them as they are to be hired. It can feel like your résumé has been dumped down a cosmic job search black hole.

  "Hey, Bud, I sent in my résumé a week ago and I haven't heard anything yet! What should I do?"

  So… what to do? First of all, it's typical for a company to take *weeks* to respond to résumé and applications. When and if they do respond, it may be only to inform you that someone will be calling you for a phone interview. Then, maybe a week later someone does actually call for a phone interview.

Assuming you get through the phone interview to the next level (which is not a given in today's job market), you may wait a week or two… or three… just to get an invitation to the first round of on-site, in-person interviews.

Some of my clients weren't hired until several months after they first applied for a position.

The waiting game feels like a dirty trick. Don't these people know the suspense is killing you? They know, I guess, but clearly don't care. Sorry.

Keep your pipeline full. Just because you applied to a place today doesn't mean you now sit around twiddling your thumbs, staring at the phone like a dumped lover, waiting futilely for the call that will never come. Submit your résumé. Continue on with your search. If they call, they call. That's all you can do.

We haven't even mentioned online application processes, another dirty trick devised by sadistic job search devils. You can't talk to a live human being. You can't send in a résumé. You can't ask questions. You can't even proceed to the next item until you complete the dreaded "How much did you make in your last job?" question.

Expect some frustrations in the job search. Most importantly, keep your head right! Stay focused and upbeat. Keep your energy positive. Don't let little obstacles bring you down. Of course, some obstacles will not only challenge your patience, they will challenge your ethics.

Lying to Get a Job

A little white lie can get you a job; at least, that's the case according to some people. On the other hand, we already know that the people telling us this are willing to lie!

A colleague in the career coaching industry sent out a quick e-mail: "One of my candidates is getting advice from more than one recruiter to say she is still with her former company... he says companies are not even talking to folks who do not currently have a job... What do you think about this issue?"

There are actually two issues here. The first one is the matter of companies "not even talking to folks who currently do not have a job."

Companies simply want the best qualified candidate, right? In a job market like this one, is it really true that people currently employed are automatically better than those who have been laid off? I don't know how common this philosophy of "only currently employed candidates" is, but it doesn't really make sense to me.

One theory put forth by another career coach is that recruiters are simply telling their candidates this, and that the companies are not really requiring it. What incentives would recruiters have to do this? Perhaps they believe it looks better to their client companies if they are providing currently employed candidates. Otherwise, the client company may think, "We can get unemployed applicants ourselves without any help from a recruiter."

In any case, there's a bigger issue here. Should you lie to get a job? Maybe not a big lie, just a little stretch? You know, minor résumé inflation, for example.

"Sure, I got laid off from ABC Company two or three months ago. However, why not just put '2006 - present' on my résumé instead of '2006 - 2010'"?

Here's some straight-forward advice: don't do it.

Why not? Even apart from your personal ethics, there is a good reason to avoid lying on a résumé.

When someone finds out your deception during the selection process – and they will find out – the credibility of every word on your résumé is in question. Even if you explain, "Oh, it was just a little oversight", the results will be damaging to your chances.

You will not get the job.

You may even find that word spreads around to other employers!

So just don't do it.

Be careful what you say on your résumé. Promote yourself. Brag on your accomplishments. Put in all the positives you can.

But don't lie.

So, there may be challenges to your patience or to your ethics. However, as the next topic illustrates, when it comes to challenges, there's no place like home!

Baby, I Love You – But Get Off My Back! Or, What If My Spouse is a Little Too Supportive?

At some point, support and encouragement feel a lot like, well, nagging!

"Honey, did you look for a job today? Here, I marked some classified ads for you!"

Actually, maybe you need a little accountability to get up off the sofa and get moving! A bigger problem though is this - what if your spouse is more stressed over your job situation than you?

Here's another potential scenario - your spouse wants you to get a job right away but you, down in your heart of hearts, have actually decided you're not all that interested in gainful employment at the moment.

Either way, the solution here is the same: good communication. Sounds simplistic, maybe, but it's profoundly true. During the job search, consciously build more and better communication into your marital relationship.

The effort will pay off in more peace and happiness for everyone, including you, your spouse and the kids.

Ageism and the "Over Qualified" Issue

Discrimination in hiring based on age is illegal.

However, now that we've got the niceties out of the way, let's get down to realities of the job search.

You are a baby boomer, 50 or older and looking for a new job. There's a possibility you've heard a phrase like this one:

"You're over-qualified."

Am I right?

It is a real issue that I find it to be not uncommon. Here is how to view the issue and what your strategy should be.

First of all, *over-qualified* can be a catch phrase hiding other meanings. When someone says you are over-qualified, obviously they probably have a deeper concern that they aren't admitting. The fact that a person has skills, experiences and strengths beyond those necessary for the job is a nonsensical reason not to hire them!

The first thing to do when confronted with the "you are over-qualified" excuse is to understand the interviewer's real concern. The interviewer *says*, "You are over-qualified" but what the interviewer *means* is…

1. **You will quit soon.** "I'm concerned that you will quit as soon as something better comes along and I will back at square one, trying to hire someone."

2. **You will cost more.** "You're going to be expensive (and even if you do accept a lower rate for now, as soon as something better comes along, you will quit. I will be back at square one, trying to hire someone)."

3. **You will get bored.** "You're going to get bored (and then quit, become apathetic or spend your time creating trouble). So I'm going to end up trying to motivate you, or dealing with problems you created, or you're going to quit and…."

4. **You will be a problem.** "You're experienced and a little bit older, so even if you like it here, will you be harder to boss around? Will you be harder to fire if we decide you're not working out? Will you be resistant to change? After all, you probably aren't up to snuff on current technology and computers!" (Studies indicate that Americans have deeply entrenched negative perceptions of seniors.)

If your strategy for dealing with this issue is to have any hope of success, it has to address the *unspoken concerns* of the hiring company or interview (one or more of the points above) rather than the *stated position* they are taking that you are over-qualified.

So what to do?

Sometimes a job seeker's first thought is to dumb down their résumé. I call this strategy résumé deflation, which means not including all your history, education, or skills. It's the opposite of résumé inflation, in which you add non-existent qualifications.

However, this résumé deflation could (a) leave suspicions about gaps in your résumé and (b) the "over-qualified" issue will still arise in interviews, so a dumbed-down résumé won't really deal with the problem. It could also leave you in the position of feeling like you have to say things that aren't exactly true. That's not a comfortable position and may come back to haunt you.

On the other hand, every résumé should be edited to present the qualifications that are most relevant to the particular job posting.

Side note: there are ways to de-age a résumé that are useful and legitimate. See the section in the résumé chapter, "How to De-Age Your Résumé". Also, it never hurts to present a youthful image of energy and enthusiasm in an interview.

A better strategy that applies when you do get an interview is to (a) listen carefully during the interview, (b) determine what the real objection may be and (c) give a good reply to the real objection.

Remember, the interviewer is probably thinking about one of the four concerns listed below. Attempt to provide a reason or rationale that would counter the particular concern. You may want to point out that your experience will help you (a) avoid costly mistakes, (b) reduce costs and (c) get better results, saving money and making money for the company.

1. The interviewer thinks, **"You will quit soon."**

    Your message must reassure the interviewer that you *are looking for a long-term commitment*. "I'm very interested in this position and your company. I feel there is a good fit and I am interested in being here permanently."

2. The interviewer thinks, **"You will cost more."**

Your message must reassure the interviewer that you are *more interested in fit* than the highest possible compensation.

You may want to point out, "For me, a job is more than just a pay check. It's about doing work I love with people I like. This position looks like a really good fit for me."

See Chapter 12, "Negotiate Like a Pro" for more tips. I'm not saying you shouldn't negotiate for the highest possible compensation; just that first, before the negotiation stage, you need to show that you are more interested in providing value for the company than getting the top compensation.

3. The interviewer thinks, **"You will get bored and become apathetic... or are a trouble-maker... or will quit."**

Your message must reassure the interviewer that you are an enthusiastic worker with a great attitude that is supportive of management, change and new ideas. "You know, I always find there is something new to learn at every job. I am excited about fitting in and learning as much as I can!"

4. The interviewer thinks, **"You will be a problem because you are in a protected class".**

Your best message most likely is similar to the suggestion for objection #3 above. Reassure the interviewer that you have a history of supporting management and adapting to change.

In addition, turn your liability ("too old and over-qualified") into an asset with benefits:

"I'd just like to point out that my depth of experience will help me avoid costly mistakes, reduce costs and get better results which will save money and make money for the company. You'll be hiring someone who has been tested and proven reliable!"

In review, if you think you are being viewed as over-qualified, try to determine the real underlying concerns. Then be careful to suggest answers to those objections. Finally, emphasize the benefits to the company of your maturity, experience and broad skill base.

10 Strategies for Getting Started

There are a lot of bad ways to get fired. I was fired on my birthday. I know people who worked at a major corporation for 30 years and received the news they were fired *on a conference call*. Getting fired is painful and you will go through a normal grieving process.

Bottom line is this: the longer it takes you to start moving forward, the harder it is to get moving at all. Notice I didn't say, "The longer it takes you to get over it". Fact is, it may take while to get over it. I found myself still nursing my wounds two years down the road after being let go. You *don't* have to get over it right away, but you *do* need to start moving right away or you will bog down in a psychological tarpit of inertia.

So here are 10 strategies for getting started...

1. Learn about and apply for unemployment.

2. Write your transition statement (see the section in this chapter called "What Happened?").

3. Review your financial position.

4. Make financial adjustments with the expectation of the job searching for 6 months.

5. Put aside the project or "honey do" list. Your first project is to land your next job and that will take full-time effort!

6. Psychologically embrace the job search as your new job. Devote a significant amount of time to it each week, 30+ hours. Make it your priority!

7. Set up a specific area of your home – your official job search "office" - with a chair, table or desk, phone, computer, lamp, calendar, paper and pencils.

8. Set a schedule for your job search activities – office hours! And stick to them!

9. Make a list of job search "Things to Do" and prioritize them.

10. Put down this book, go start – right now!

Five Strategies for Keeping Yourself Motivated

Here are five strategies that will help you keep your head right and stay motivated during your job search.

1. Enlist a support group or buddy – somebody to meet with regularly for a cup of coffee and a listening ear.

2. Turn off the T.V news if it's depressing, as well as any other sources of discouragement.

3. Monitor and manage your self-talk.

4. Reconnect with your spiritual resources.

5. Develop traits of psychological resilience:

    a. View your circumstances as a *challenge* rather than a threat.

    b. Move out of the denial phase and *commit* to the job search.

    c. Break out of helplessness and take *control* of your life by focusing on steps you can take now.

Five Strategies for Staying Focused

Maintaining the right attitude is not only a matter of encouraging yourself, it is also about staying focused on your daily job search activities and weekly job search goals. Here are five strategies that will help you to stay focused and keep you moving forward.

1. Create a marketing plan - daily and weekly schedules and lists of job search items to do: mailing out résumés, making networking calls and appointments, searching job boards, contacting recruiters, targeting companies and researching them, etc.

2. Use a variety of techniques in your job search; don't just look on the internet.

3. Set S.M.A.R.T. goals.

4. Create accountability systems, such as "to do" lists.

5. Hire a career coach; preferably, me!

2

Get Organized

The job search process in any economy is difficult but it's more so when times are tough. Frankly, finding the job you want in a reasonably timely manner is not likely to happen unless you stay focused, get organized and conduct an all-out campaign. This chapter provides the strategies you need to organize yourself for success.

What You Need to Do IMMEDIATELY After Losing Your Job

There are five things you need to do immediately after losing your job:

1. Decide about Cobra

2. Apply for unemployment.

3. Create a transition budget.

4. Determine the minimum and maximum income you must have from your next job.

5. Organize your home office.

Each of the following sections will give you some basic background information you need and outline steps to get you going. Get started today!

Decide About Cobra

The Consolidated Omnibus Budget Reconciliation Act of 1985, or **COBRA**, is a federal law that gives the right to continue health insurance coverage after leaving employment.

Basically, COBRA provides certain former employees, retirees, spouses, former spouses and dependent children the right to temporary continuation of health coverage at group rates. However, generally the expense will be more than you were contributing as an employee because your employer was carrying part of the cost. Still, continuing with your existing group rates is likely to be less expensive than purchasing individual coverage.

If you feel you *can't* afford COBRA (and most people who are qualified probably don't use the benefit because of the cost), you have to decide what you *will* do about basic health insurance. You may decide to get quotes on individual coverage. It's not in the scope of this book to make suggestions about your health insurance coverage but you do need to look into the matter and determine your best strategy for approaching it.

You can find more information at the Department of Labor website, www.dol.gov. The URL for Frequently Asked Questions is www.dol.gov/ebsa/faqs/faq_consumer_cobra.html.

Apply for Unemployment

You also need to file for unemployment immediately after losing your job. Some people let embarrassment hold them back. There is no need to feel ashamed – the funds exist for the purpose of helping in situations like yours. You've been paying your taxes, so claim your benefits.

You may not even need to go down to the unemployment office. In many states, you can apply on-line or over the phone. Go to your state government website and you should be able to find the contact information there.

Create a Transition Budget

The next thing you must do is get a grip on your financial situation. This is the time and arena to be conservative, not optimistic. Plan on your transition lasting *at least* six months. Take into account the difference between your new unemployment income and your previous fully employed income.

Decide what luxuries you may need to reduce in order to live on your new income. Please do not do something stupid such as withdrawing money from your retirement funds. Instead, figure out how to live within the limits of your new means.

Determine Your Income Needs

While you are working on your transition budget, you may as well go ahead and do just a little more thinking about money. Now is the time to set your income targets for your next job. There are two questions you need to answer:

1. What is the *lowest* total compensation I would accept for an otherwise perfect job?

2. What is the *target* total compensation I am targeting?

One aspect of good negotiating is simply to be sure you *know what a win is*. Determine now what your minimum and maximum compensation expectations are so you will be prepared in the negotiating phase of the job search to know a win when you find it.

7 Strategies for Organizing Your Home Office

Ready to organize your home office? Here are some steps to consider:

1. Even if you will use the computer at the library, set up a home office for your job search.

2. Get the supplies you need including pens, notepaper, résumé paper, envelopes and thank you cards.

3. Get the equipment you need: desk or table space, phone, fax and printer.

4. Consider whether you need faster internet service and a different cell phone service.

5. If you use more than one résumé, give each résumé a name, put a copy of it in a separate file and then keep a list of the employers to whom you send that résumé in the file.

6. Set up a file called "Networking". You can also use readily available software like Microsoft Outlook.

7. Collect the information you will need for applications, résumés and your first day on the job once hired.

3

Step Back, Take Stock and Think Strategically

"So what do you want to do when you grow up," jokingly asked my sister. Can't blame her, I was 50 years old and in career transition – again!

After working with hundreds of career transition clients, I know from their own words that one of the blessings in disguise of forced career transition is the opportunity to reassess one's career and re-evaluate one's career plans and goals. Once you have landed in your next position, you may very well find yourself thankful that you had the opportunity to change direction and make choices that you probably never would have if your previous career had continued uninterrupted.

Therefore, avoid the temptation of thinking, "Well, I will just take anything." That's *not* a good strategy for multiple reasons:

- You're cheating yourself of an opportunity to do something you will really love.

- It's actually harder to find a job without a career focus than it is to aim at something relatively specific.

- Your best advantages in landing a position are your experiences, strengths, skills and accomplishments but they won't necessarily apply to "just anything".

So do yourself a great favor – shake off the doubt and discouragement and decide to target a career field that excites you!

Aim at Something!

Fire! Ready! Aim!

That's the way some people start their career transition – firing off résumés in massive amounts to any job posting that looks remotely interesting! It doesn't work for shooting a gun and it's not a useful way of conducting your job search. Here's the right way:

Ready! – Take time to consider your experiences, strengths, skills and past accomplishments. List them. Do some soul-searching. What industry and career field do you wish to pursue? What kind of company do you want to work for? What are your financial constraints? Are you willing to relocate? How far are you willing to commute?

Aim! – Put it all together. Write down your target, the perfect job. What industry? What kind of company? What position? What pay? Located where?

Fire! – No, you may not find that "perfect" job that you targeted. You may have to make some compromises. However, I can tell you a 100 percent guaranteed way to not find the perfect job – don't aim for it!

Résumé Blasting Does Not Work

My clients ask me about some of the services that blast résumés out and even fax them to thousands of companies and guarantee interviews. I have been told there are several sources that have consistently pegged the rate of return on a generic résumé blast at 0.6 percent. In practical terms, that suggests that if you send out 500 résumés, expect three responses.

My advice – don't waste your time, energy and money blasting résumés.

10 Career Planning Strategies

Here are ten strategies for thinking strategically about your job search.

1. Reconnect with your personal mission and look for work that taps into your interests, even something about which you can be passionate!

2. Assess your strengths. Write down the top three to five.

3. Assess your preferred working environment. Do you want to work in a small, medium or large business? In a formal or informal environment? Or even at home?

4. Assess your personality. There are many personality inventories online or available through professional career coaches.

5. Assess your motivations. What drives your engine? Achievement? Personal satisfaction? Financial rewards? Opportunity for advancement?

6. Assess the job market. What industries are growing? What career fields are in demand?

7. Research potential new career fields. Track down and talk to someone in a growing career field that interests you. What does it take to get into that line of work?

8. Evaluate educational opportunities. Consider going back to school.

9. Write your career plan.

10. Research salary norms in your career field and target job titles.

Four Strategies for Figuring Out What You Want and Need (Self-assessment)

1. Assess your **life and career values** using The Work Importance Locator on O*NET: www.onetcenter.org/WIL.html.

2. Assess your **career interests** using The Interest Profiler on O*NET: www.onetcenter.org/IP.html.

3. Assess your **skills and competencies** using the survey on the Skills Search page of O*NET: http://online.onetcenter.org/skills.

4. Assess your **personality traits** using any number of free, online assessments, several of which are listed below. Many personality assessment sites offer a *free* version and an upgraded *fee* version.

    a. www.careerkey.org
    b. www.humanmetrics.com/#Jung%20Myers-Briggs
    c. www.assessment.com

Three Strategies for Figuring Out the Best Opportunities (Market-assessment)

1. Use the online **Occupational Outlook Handbook** (http://www.bls.gov/oco), which will tell you the training and education needed, earnings, expected job prospects, what workers do on the job and working conditions for hundreds of different types of jobs.

2. Use the online **America's Career Information Net** sponsored by the Department of Labor (http://www.acinet.org/acinet/default.asp) which provides occupational, demographic and labor market information at the local, state and national levels.

3. Want to find potential new occupations based on skills and knowledge similar to those used in your current or previous job? You should check out **mySkillsmyFuture** at www.myskillsmyfuture.org. Sponsored by the U.S. Department of Labor, it will help you find occupations that require skills and knowledge similar to your current or previous job. In addition, you can learn more about these suggested matches, locate local training programs, and/or apply for actual job postings. The site is interactive, easy to use and like the other websites listed in this section - free!

4. Use your personal networking skills on the professional networking site www.linkedin.com to get lots of insider perspective and information.

Two Strategies for Managing Your Money During Your Job Search (Financial-assessment)

1. Just sit down and do a budget. It's not sexy, but it will help you make the necessary decisions to navigate the financial shoals of a career transition.

2. I recommend the tools and resources of Crown Financial Ministries for all your financial strategizing needs (www.crown.org/tools).

Hope is not a strategy.
~Rudy Giuiliani~

4

Learn the Tools of the Trade and Use Them

I dashed off a quick e-mail to one of my job search clients:

> Jill:
>
> I don't know if you had a chance to meet and negotiate with Air Products yet, but thought I would suggest this - once you do reach an agreement with them (or any other company) and an offer has been presented and accepted, it's usually a good idea to sit down immediately afterward and send **a confirmation letter** to the interviewer. The purpose of the letter would be to say thank you"– which is always appropriate – but also to put in writing everything to which you agreed. It's simply good business, especially if your salary and benefits negotiations included anything out of the ordinary. You never know when the documentation may come in handy.

Confirmation letters are just one of several tools of the job search trade. This chapter contains a list and brief description of this and other essential items you need in your job search toolkit.

The Basics

Online Applications

When you apply for a job you may be asked to complete an employment application even if you have already submitted a résumé and cover letter. It's important for your job applications to be complete, accurate and error free. Here is the information you may need to take with you to complete an application for employment. I suggest putting it all on a piece of paper to take with you. Then just copy the items you need onto the application.

Job Application Form Items

Personal Information:
- Address
- City, state, zip code
- Phone number
- Eligibility to work in US
- Felony convictions

Education:
- Schools/colleges attended
- Major
- Degree/diploma
- Graduation dates(s)

Position Applied For Information:
- Title of the job you are applying for
- Hours/days available to work
- When you can start work

Employment Information:
- Names, addresses and phone numbers of previous employers
- Former supervisor's name
- Dates of employment
- Salary
- Reason for leaving

References
- List of three references - names, job title or relationship, addresses and phone numbers

Résumé (if you have one)

The information above lists items you need to take with you. The next section lists important things to remember when you complete the application.

Do's and Don't for Completing Job Applications

#1   **Don't leave anything blank.** Take the application home and return it when it's completed, if necessary.

#2   **Do write clearly and neatly.** Use black or blue ink.

#3   **Do keep it neat and clean.** If you mess up, ask for a new application form and start over.

#4   **Do check for spelling and grammatical errors.** Always proofread your job application form before turning it in.

#5   **Do list your most recent job first** when completing employment information.

#6   **Do list your most recent education first.** Include vocational schools, training programs, colleges attended and the high school from which you graduated.

#7   **Do ask permission of anyone you intend to name as a reference.** References don't necessarily have to be professional. If you have volunteered, you can use members of the organizations that you have helped or students can use teachers.

Résumés

The "old gray résumé" ain't what she used to be!

Pulling out a résumé from three or four years ago, adding your last employment information and using it like that probably is *not* a good idea.

The biggest understatement in this book – you need a good résumé. Other than personal recommendations and connections through your personal and professional network, your résumé is the number one way to get an interview.

If you don't get any interviews, you won't get a job. If you don't have an outstanding résumé, you won't get interviews. Therefore, if you don't have an outstanding résumé, you won't get a job.

In a good economy, a great résumé is very important. In a bad economy, a great résumé is absolutely essential. Notice I did not say a "good" résumé... instead, a *great* résumé!

We've got a whole chapter designed to help you determine if your résumé is a great one but here are the essential basics of any résumé designed to make you stand out from the crowd:

1. It must contain no errors of fact or grammar.
2. It must be easy to read.
3. It must present your skills, strengths and experiences in a clear and impactful way.

As we said, there's more information later on concerning your résumé.

Cover Letters

Cover letters and cover emails are the same thing. If you attach your résumé to an email, the email needs to contain the same content you would put in a hard copy cover letter.

Of course, you will need different letters with slightly different content for different job search events. Here's the key – any cover letter you send should enhance without repeating verbatim from the résumé a few noteworthy qualities and achievements that make you an outstanding candidate.

However, keep it brief! The cover letter has one purpose only – make the reader curious enough to take a glance at your résumé. The cover letter is not an exhaustive list or an essay!

Finally, at the end of any cover letter, request an interview or meeting. If possible, proactively schedule a follow-up call. Be sure to follow through!

Thank You Notes

It's always appropriate to thank people for their help and time. Good manners and common sense both suggest you are going to need some thank you notes to use throughout your job search.

I say "good manners" because it's, well, good manners… "Common sense" because job search today is an effort to market "brand you"… and every time a person receives one of your handwritten "thank you notes", it's a reminder of the classy person you are, deserving any job search help the recipient can provide.

Here are a few times it is appropriate to send a handwritten, hard copy thank you note:

- Someone passed along your name to a potential employer.

- Someone granted an informational interview.

- Always send a thank you to your interviewers – do it immediately following the interview! Regardless of how well you believe the interview went, it is appropriate to thank the interviewer for their time.

Actually, let's get to the point – you need help in your job search. In one way or another, many people will likely give you some kind of help. Take time to say, "Thanks!"

Emails

Should you send your résumé via e-mail? Should you send a thank you via email? If you send your résumé via email, should you write an email cover letter? Can you use an email to follow up on a job interview?

You can do all of the above. E-mail has become ubiquitous. Everybody uses it. So use it. However, there is a danger which can be summed up simply – over-familiarity.

Here are a few basic guidelines for using e-mail in your job search activities without falling prey to over-familiarity:

- Get a professional sounding e-mail address for your job search. Your friends may know that "dirtydaniel" refers to your love of gardening or that "partygirl18" refers to your fondness for formal dinner parties. Potential employers may draw their own, less impressive conclusions. So set up a boring, professional e-mail address such as firstinitial and lastname.

- If you send an e-mail, keep an air of formality about it. Write the content using wording you would normally use in a hard copy letter.

"Brag Books" and Portfolios

Many sales professionals maintain a brag book that they bring to interviews. The brag book is a portfolio containing documentation of awards and achievements. The practice is becoming more common among other professions and you may want to consider creating one.

You can find an appropriate, professional looking binding at most office supply stores. Organize each item in a protective covering. Include the following types of items.

Documents demonstrating achievements
- Awards/honors
- Business achievements and experiences (such as team member awards)
- Certificates of appreciation
- Letters of recommendation and references
- Performance reviews
- Positive evaluations/comments from persons attending your presentations, training sessions or workshops
- Thank you notes and cards from corporate clients or individuals

Documents demonstrating job-relevant skills
- Artwork and photographs
- Graphic design aamples
- Articles
- Business reports
- Computer skills and courses completed
- Lesson plans and samples of student work
- Marketing materials
- Speeches (either written for someone else or personally delivered)

Documents demonstrating training, education and qualifications
- Academic degrees/honors
- Certificates from any continuing education, including courses, training, seminars, workshops or conferences
- Licenses or certifications

Of course, include any other professional materials that demonstrate you achievements, skills, education or qualifications. Take the portfolio with you to interviews and use it at appropriate moments for show and tell. Just make sure it is neat, organized and impressive!

Informational Interviews

You may not be familiar with the concept of an informational interview. Basically, it just means talking with people to get information about an occupation or industry. It's a great way of expanding your network, too!

In an informational interview, your goal is just what the name suggests – obtaining information, not asking for a job. It is perfectly appropriate to contact people you know or to whom you've been recommended and ask them for a short appointment to learn more about their career field or industry.

Of course, in today's environment of e-mail and voice mail it can be difficult to get an opportunity to speak with a person on the phone and ask for the appointment personally. When you do succeed, remember that time is precious and keep your meeting short – about 15 or 20 minutes unless invited to stay longer.

The informational interview is well-known and understood in the job market and many people actually feel honored that you would want to stop by and ask a few questions.

Go prepared. Here a few of the kinds of things you can learn and ask about:

- How would you describe a typical day at work?
- What is the potential for growth in this field?
- What should I do next to help find employment in this field?

Remember: send a thank you card!

Business Cards

You can get a limited number of free business cards online at sites like www.vistaprint.com. You're going to be meeting a lot of people. Go ahead and get some cards. They don't have to state a job title or company name! Your name and contact information will do. They'll look more professional and save you countless times of writing your name and phone number on some piece of scrap paper!

Job Boards, Company Websites and Job Search Engines

Job boards are internet sites to which you can upload your résumé. The biggest national job boards are Monster, Career Builder and Hot Jobs. There are also local job boards (www.chattanoogahasjobs.com, for example.) There are also specialty or "niche" job boards, such as www.dice.com for the IT industry. In addition to job seekers posting their résumés there, companies also post job openings there.

Recruiters can search these boards for qualified applicants. Job boards have virtually replaced job postings in the classified ad sections of newspapers. However, posting your résumé to a job board is definitely not a cure all! The challenge is to present a résumé that will stand out from the hundreds, thousands, or hundreds of thousands of other résumés on a board!

Further, there is a growing trend away from job boards among hiring companies and recruiters. Social media (such as the professional networking site www.linkedin.com) or even the purely social networking sites (www.facebook.com) are being used as job search tools. Still, posting a résumé to job boards is a viable job search strategy. Don't think that simply posting your résumé is a sufficient job search strategy; it is not!

Companies also post jobs on their **company websites**. In a bad economy where the number of candidates is plentiful – or even overwhelming – companies have shown a tendency to abandon the job boards and simply post openings on their websites.

Targeting companies, researching them, locating their websites, uploading your résumé and then following up appropriately is a strategy that can be effective.

Job search engines are websites on which you can type in the kind of job you are looking for and the website will give you all the results it finds on the internet. Actually, these sites are online databases which mine the Internet for job openings and aggregate them for your convenience. Many job boards also feature a job search engine. One of the best general job search engines is www.indeed.com.

Recruiters and Agencies

Recruiters are often the best link to jobs, especially higher paying ones. However, you really need to understand that there are different types of recruiters, how they work and strategies for getting the best results from them.

Corporate Recruiters are employees of a company who locate candidates to fill positions in their company and manage the pre-selection process.

Retained Recruiters/Executive Search Firms are third party professionals retained by a client company to work exclusively on a candidate search, usually for higher-level positions with annual salaries of $150,000 or more. These are the true head-hunters. They are paid by the company who contracts with them, regardless of whether a placement is made. A retained recruiter may take a very active role in the marketing of a candidate to a company.

Contingency Recruiters work for *Search Firms.* Like retained recruiters, they are third party professionals but they generally perform the search for individual contributor and middle management levels. Their agreement with the company is non-exclusive – there may be other contingency recruiters seeking to fill the same position for the company – so their compensation is contingent upon providing the candidate ultimately chosen to fill the position.

Staffing Agencies are actually employers. They hire you and then place you in temporary, part-time or even full-time jobs of limited or permanent duration with one of their client companies. The client company pays the agency; the agency pays you. Some positions offered by the staffing agency may be temp-to-perm, meaning that after an initial period (for example, 90 days) the staffing agency may agree to release you from their employment and the client company may hire you on as a regular employee.

Placement Agencies and Private Career Consultants charge you a fee to assist you in finding a position. As with the purchase of any service, investigate and ensure that you understand exactly what level of assistance you are getting for your money. You *never pay* a recruiter *except* in the case of fees charged by placement agencies or private career consultants!

Every state has a *State Employment Agency* which will provide job listings, employment counseling and perhaps other related help. Services are free.

Advanced Tools

Executives, senior managers and other professionals may use more advanced job search tools, such as biographies, blogs, online résumés and videos. In addition, anyone can use some of the newer job search tools now available and gaining popularity, such as job match sites and social networking media.

Your Personal Brand

I once heard a speaker state, "You don't want to be just another chocolate chip in the chocolate chip factory."

In the competitive job market, you can't *afford* to be another chocolate chip in the chocolate chip factory. You must stand out in order to get noticed. The way to do that is through personal branding.

Business guru Tom Peters was the first to make the point, "To be in business today, our most important job is to be head marketer for the brand called You."

Biographies

Executive-level job seekers may find a personal biography to be a useful tool in the place of a résumé. A well-written bio can help key decision-makers quickly understand who you are and what you have accomplished. In addition, biographies are well-adapted to presentation by electronic media.

Blogs

Blogging is a great way – perhaps the best way – of establishing and managing your online presence, which is essential in today's job search. My colleague Kristen Jacoway of www.reach.org is a career design coach and she helps people and entrepreneurs / small business owners define their personal brands, establish their social media / Internet marketing positions, and make career moves to achieve their goals. You can find her at www.careerdesigncoach.com.

According to Kristen, there are the four common blog platforms.

Four Common Blog Platforms
by Kristen Jacoway

Wordpress.com - is free and is hosted on their domain. The pro and the con is there is no customization of code--you can use it almost like MS Word - it's very much WYSIWYG (what you see is what you get). So, if you are not comfortable with coding, this is a good platform. If you want to customize your code, you'll be very limited here with the functionality and customization options (i.e. themes, plug-ins, etc.). It makes it a little harder to integrate social media for those reasons.

Wordpress.org - This is the self-hosted version of WordPress. It is free, but you will install it on your own domain (i.e. GoDaddy, Blue Host, DreamHost, MediaTemple, JustHost, Laughing Squid, etc). Because it is on your domain, you control your content and your SEO (search engine optimization).

At this writing, WordPress.org has 36 pages of free themes built inside the control panel, but if you wanted a premium theme or a theme developed by a certain designer, you will have to upload it to the administrative panel. It is open-source (anything that is created to be used by the general public and free to modify), so there is a wide variety of themes and plug-ins available to increase your site's functionality. It's a great base for social media because of all the plug-ins that are available for use with it.

Typepad.com -They have several apps and widgets you can integrate into the site. It's pretty straightforward and you can do customization of your banner to upload on this site.

I have hosted my blog and website here and really like how easy it is to use. You do pay a monthly fee for the service, but this gives you access to customer service. They have a tremendous knowledge base that you can search and find the answer to almost any question you have about how to do something.

You can point a domain name to the site. I recommend using GoDaddy for this as it is really easy to do. The knowledge base has step-by-step directions and screenshots on how to do it. I actually have my own name, www.kristenjacoway.com, as well as the URL www.careerdesigncoach.com pointing to my TypePad® website / blog. As part of developing online identity and thought leadership, it's recommended to buy your own name as the domain name. TypePad® offers service at different levels depending on what you want to do and ranges from beginner / basic all the way up to someone who is familiar with coding and CSS (Cascading Style Sheets).

Blogger.com - Owned by Google, is free, and is hosted on their domain, so you are bound by their terms and service agreement. It is a basic blogging platform and no customization of code is required for this site, so you will not be able to customize the look and feel of the blog.

Online Videos and Résumés

YouTube videos are beginning to become part of the job interviewing process for some positions!

A job search coach told me of one of her clients who was applying for a position involving delivering product presentations and workshops.

The company instructed him to open an account on YouTube and put a video of him actually delivering a presentation for them to view. He sent them the logon and password once he was ready. The only contact prior to this was a phone screen and emails.

Since then, I have heard of similar requirements in other situations!

Also, some executives are now preparing video résumés which can also be posted on-line.

Job Match Websites

Another relatively recent development includes job match websites. These websites differ from traditional job search engines in that they use your résumé and other information to match your skills and objectives with specific job postings. Prime examples include:

www.jobfox.com

www.trovix.com

www.realmatch.com

Four Strategies for Overcoming Techno-phobia

Are the Internet and computers big mysteries to you? Rather pull a tooth than surf the web? Never check e-mail? Don't care anything about websites?

You, my friend, are a techno-phobe! Don't feel bad – so are lots of other people.

Here's the bad news for you: there's no way to avoid using a computer in today's job search! Even the simplest job application processes generally require an online or computer-based application.

However, here's the good news – computers and the Internet are easy. Besides that, you've got to catch up to times at some point and frankly, that point is now! Three strategies for getting comfortable with the technology of the job search:

1. Read a book like "The Internet for Dummies."

2. Take a computer course at a local community college.

3. Read Chapter 5: "Master the Computer and Maximize the Web."

4. Ask your kids or young niece or nephew to teach you – just make them slow down so you can follow what they are doing!

4 Strategies for Using Recruiters

How do you work with a recruiter effectively? Start by locating recruiters that may interest you. The best way to locate a good recruiter is by asking your network for referrals.

However, you can also use Internet sites such as www.recruitersdirectory.com or your local Yellow Pages. After submitting your résumé and cover letter, you'll be contacted by the recruiter if she believes you may fit a position she's filling.

Remember that recruiters work for their client company, not for you!

Do NOT be surprised if your recruiter initially shows some interest and then drops you like a hot potato! If a recruiter does not see you as a potential fit for a position she is currently filling, it may be next to impossible to reach the recruiter by phone.

With that in mind, here are effective strategies for working with recruiters.

1. Treat your recruiter ***professionally*** at all times.

    a. Respond to phone calls and interviews as though the recruiter were an actual employer.

    b. Do not mislead the recruiter about critical information such as your desired salary range or the fact that you are working with other recruiters.

    c. Prepare for your initial interview with a potential recruiter.

    d. Send only a polished and professional résumé and other materials to your recruiter.

2. Treat your recruiter as you would a ***trusted partner.***

    a. Speaking of trust – rely on your instincts – don't work with a recruiter you don't trust.

    b. Attempt to learn as much as you can about a recruiter before committing to him or her.

    c. As mentioned above, be appropriately open and honest with your recruiter.

     d. Hold up your end of the bargain – respond quickly to your recruiter and prepare well for any interviews your recruiter arranges for you. Keep the recruiter informed of progress made.

     e. When you receive an offer from a firm, make your decision in a timely manner – no more than three days – so that your recruiter doesn't look bad to the client company.

3. Understand *your recruiter's motivations* and respond accordingly.

     a. The company is paying the recruiter, not you. Your recruiter is primarily concerned that the client company perceives you to be an excellent candidate.

     b. The recruiter may ask for the names of firms where you've already interviewed. They want the information to market their services to the firms you mention. Simply reply that prior to forwarding your résumé to a position, they can ask if you have previously spoken with the client company and you will be glad to let them know at that time.

4. Use your recruiter **strategically**.

     a. Your recruiter can help you determine a realistic compensation range to expect from any firm the recruiter is representing.

     b. Your recruiter can help you prepare for and in some cases conduct your compensation negotiations with the hiring firm.

c.   Should you determine to reject an offer outright, let your recruiter know in advance.

d.   Don't burn bridges with your recruiters. You may need their help later on!

e.   A recruiter can be a great partner, but it's your job search. So use recruiters wisely but don't abdicate responsibility to them for your success. That will always be up to you!

Have thy tools ready. God will find thee work.
~Charles Kingsley~

5

Master the Computer and Maximize the Web

The Wall Street Journal published an article entitled ***Beyond Job Boards*** that highlights some recent trends in career transition.[iii] Here are some of the findings:

- Companies are scaling back online job board advertising (thus saving money) and are focusing more on their own company website career pages.

- Companies report that people applying through their websites are on average better-qualified than applicants coming through job boards.

- Many job seekers are finding success by first networking with employees at the company via social media like LinkedIn and then applying directly with the company instead of through the job boards.

- Visitors searching for work on job boards have increased 37 percent from a year earlier (suggesting that competition for job postings is very high).

- And… among the most successful new hires are those referred by existing employees.

The 2007 Recruiting Trends Survey sponsored by Direct Employers Association collects information from 50 talent acquisition and management practitioners who represent leading companies across several industries.[iv] Key findings from that survey include:

- Fifty-five percent of new hires were sourced from the internet in 2006, a number that reflects approximately eight percent growth over our 2005 results.

- The majority of recruitment dollars are being spent on advertising and posting on general job boards; however, satisfaction with the return on investment from this source appears to be relatively low. In line with these findings, respondents indicated, in open-responses, a growing frustration with general job boards due to financial and management costs.

- In relative terms, employee referrals and organizational websites were perceived to provide the best return on investment for respondent organizations.

The bottom line – just going online and posting your résumé on a general job board such as Monster is no longer an adequate use of the Internet in a serious job search!

Will Social Media Replace Job Boards?

In an article entitled *7-Eleven's New and Improved Sourcing Strategy: Will Social Media Replace Job Boards?*, author Madeline Laurano showed how 7-Eleven began actively measuring the effectiveness of job boards like Monster and CareerBuilder.[v] 7-Eleven reportedly was filling 128 open positions at the time and was spending $500,000 yearly on job boards, begging the question, "Is this worth it?"

7-Eleven discovered that the cost of using job boards was rising and that the quality of candidates they were receiving was declining. Beside that, their 10 recruiters were suffering from résumé overload.

In short, they were paying a lot of money, getting too many under-qualified candidates and too few well-qualified ones.

7-Eleven changed strategies. They are now engaging and connecting with candidates through a social media strategy including LinkedIn, Facebook and Twitter. They are also now updating their own career website. Finally, although the role of social media will be expanded in their recruitment and talent acquisition efforts, social media will not replace the job boards. What it will do is help 7-Eleven decide what job boards to use. Still, the message to job seekers is that more and more corporations will move some of their job search efforts away from the traditional job boards and more to social media, particularly LinkedIn.

Laurano concludes her article by saying,

> Two realities have emerged in today's talent acquisition environment. To start, companies are placing heavy emphasis on "quality" candidates and the job boards simply are not producing results. Secondly, social media has afforded companies options to expand their reach and improve their brand.

The move toward social media for recruiting is one more reason to master the computer and maximize the Web for job search success. At the very minimum, you really need to consider using LinkedIn to create and maintain an online presence for professional networking.

Are You LinkedIn?

At first, John was skeptical about using his time to create a great profile on www.linkedin.com. It's not that he was against the site, just that he didn't see any value in it.

I explained that www.linkedin.com is not a simple social networking site. It is a professional networking site which provides multiple uses for online networking, especially during a job search. Finally, John agreed to create a profile.

The next time we talked, John said, "Guess what? I was talking to a recruiter today and he told me that the first thing he does after getting a résumé is check the person's LinkedIn profile!"

Now John's a LinkedIn user and doing everything he can to optimize his profile.

If you are not familiar with www.linkedin.com, try it. The basic free membership is all you really need so there is no cost except for your time.

However, remember that this will become a very public presentation of your career. When you do create a profile, be thorough and accurate. As with your résumé, no misspelled words allowed!

Go beyond just the basic profile and do your best to invite recommendations. They can make a big difference.

That recruiter may be deciding whether or not to call you right now, so make sure you have a LinkedIn profile he can go to for additional information about you!

Of course, the Internet has its challenges and there are dangers, although a good dose of common sense can help you avoid many of them. As I will describe below, be aware of Internet job scams and be careful to protect your private information.

Internet Job Scams

Here's an example of an actual unedited bogus job offer my client Ricky Gonzalez received via email:[vi]

> The position of Assistant Director
> From: **Emeli Linstrum**
> Sent: Fri 6/19/09 12:28 AM
> To: RICKY GONZALEZ

Dear RICKY,

I represent recruiting company 1st Class Recruitment specialized in searching the candidates at the request of employers all over the world.

There is a position available at the moment offered by European company. Please see below a short description of this position.

Assistant Director

I'm pleased to offer you a part time employment as a representative of European company, interested in expanding the business to the US market. The company will create the web site oriented to the US customers with high revenues guaranteed by the complex of high-performance promotional measures. In spite of the project's intricate, your duties will be quite easy to perform. No special education or experience are required from your side. Your personal manager will lead you step by step to the success by providing you with detailed and quite easy to understand instructions. This position has a very high potential in a personal income boost as a result of business growing all in all.

The minimum salary at this position is $30,000/year (5 from the project revenues). There are no fees to pay from your side.

As a part-time position it will take only 7-9 hours a week to perform the duties.

The same time the company offers you a long term business relationship that is definitely very important in difficult times of financial crisis, because it means a guarantee of getting a stable income regardless of the situation on the labour-market.

To ask for detailed description including duties and responsibilities of the position just respond to this offer with the following subject:

"Interested in getting the position of Assistant Director."

or in case you don't like this offer for any reason, please let me know and I'll try to find something else for you.

Sincerely,
Emelie Linstrum, HR Agent
1st Class Recruitment
Gjorwellsgatan 28, 112 60
Stockholm, Sweden
+46-08-369 80 781
info@1stclassrecruitment.com

Ricky wanted to know if this offer – a lot like other offers he received regularly – was a scam. What do you think? Here is my reply to him:

In regard to the email about the assistant director position, I have to go with the old adage, "If it sounds too good to be true, it probably is". The e-mail claims you will make $30,000 yearly working one day (seven to nine hours) each week. My guess is that most likely it is a scam of some sort. They may just want to collect e-mail addresses. More likely, they will try to get you involved with them and then at some point, contrary to what is in the e-mail, you will be asked to pay a fee, send them some kind of investment or buy some kind of training.

My advice would be to do what you have been doing - just ignore these kinds of e-mails.

Four Ways to Keep Your Online Information Safe

The giant job board Monster announced in January 2009 that massive quantities of their members' personal information including names, sex, phone numbers and e-mail addresses had been stolen. The loss of personal information underlines a continuing danger of the Internet (and not restricted to the use of the Internet for job searching): the danger of identity theft.

While you must use the Internet for your job search, you must also use appropriate strategies for keeping personal information secure. The balance that you must strike is this – finding ways to restrict the amount of personal information you publish on the Internet in order to maintain security, yet giving sufficient information to make it easy for potential employers to find you.

Here are strategies for keeping your online information safe:

1. Consider the level of security you select when posting your résumé on Monster or other job boards. For example, your choices on Monster include:

    a. Public résumé – widest access to job opportunities – viewable by employers, but not other Monster members.

    b. Confidential résumé – confidential e-mail address, the job seeker sees the listing and decides whether to respond.

    c. Privacy Plus – blocks up to 20 companies from finding your public résumé (in case you have concerns about your current employer discovering your résumé is posted).

2. You can choose to use disposable or generic contact information on your résumé.

a. NEVER list your social security number on your résumé or profile.
b. Create an e-mail address (using gmail, yahoo or msn hotmail) just for the job search so you can cancel it later.
c. Do not use your full name.
d. Do not list your P.O. box.
e. List your current employer or job position generically, such as "major pharmaceutical company" or "multi-state marketing manager".

3. Read the privacy policies on social networking sites such as Facebook. Be aware that companies are **not** required to notify you if they change their privacy policies!

4. The general principle is never share private information online, such as
    a. Date of birth
    b. Social security number
    c. Bank accounts
    d. Driver's license number
    e. Credit card information
    f. PayPal account number
    g. Mother's maiden name

The website www.Privacyrights.org lists data breaches. There are a lot of them and it may be a little unsettling but knowledge is power. The Internet presents its dangers, so be safe!

Cleaning up Your Digital Dirt

Finally, there's also the issue of your online image, which is going to matter more and more in the future.

For example, many recruiters use search engines such as Google to look up prospective candidate's names. A good number of those recruiters then use what they read to eliminate a candidate from consideration!

Stories abound of people turned down for jobs because of embarrassing photos on a social networking page such as Facebook. It's not just recent graduates, either! Physicians, psychiatrists and business professionals have lost lucrative career opportunities because of their social networking page.

If your name is on the Internet, you must clean up any digital dirt that reflects poorly upon your professional image!

Here's how to get started:

1. Google your name (using quotation marks around your name, such as "Jane Doe".

2. Check images on Google and content of each entry for the first three pages on Google.

3. Contact webmasters or website owners to remove any unwanted information.

4. Bury dirt by starting a Web page or blog that is positive. As it climbs up the search results, it pushes unwanted pages further down.

5. Remove any inappropriate picture from social networking or other pages.

6. Check your privacy settings on social networking sites such as Facebook.

7. If you need help, companies such as Namyz, Feedster and Done!SEO can give your Internet image a makeover.

Give a person a fish and you feed them for a day; teach
that person to use the Internet and they won't bother
you for weeks.

~Author Unknown~

6

Understand How Companies Hire

It's easier to catch fish if you know when and where they feed. You'll have no luck casting your bait onto the shallow surface if the big ones are down in the cool depths! You may have the best bait in the world but you must put the bait where the fish are located or there will be no results.

The equivalent concept for getting a good job in a bad economy is to understand how companies hire. The main issues for the modern job hunt: (1) the use of technology and applicant tracking systems, (2) the realities of the hidden job market, and (3) the importance of networking. Finally, I'll summarize the "Top 10 Job Lead Strategies." You may need to use them all!

The Use of Technology and Applicant Tracking Systems

Applicant Tracking System (ATS) is the generic name for a database used by a company to manage the résumés it receives. Unlike days of yore, when an unsolicited résumé was (at best) immediately placed in a drawer and never seen again, today your résumé is scanned and stored electronically where it can be instantly retrieved.

Indeed, if the company experiences a job opening, they very likely will search their ATS, and should your résumé fit the key words searched for, it will appear at the top of the list. You could get a call… an interview… and a job!

Note however, that I did not say "should your résumé fit the job opening"! The issue is whether the words in your résumé match the key words that the person searches for in the database. If you understand anything about databases or even if you just know how to use Google, then you should get the point here.

Getting a good job in a bad economy means carefully observing the key words in job postings of the type that you want and making sure those words are in your résumé!

There are a host of other issues that the pervasive use of e-mail, the Internet and social media bring to the modern job search. The implications for getting a good job in a bad economy are many but the simplest lesson is this – accept the fact that you must be Internet and technology savvy to get the best jobs and don't forget to put the right keywords in your résumé!

The Hidden Job Market

You've probably seen the hidden job market operate at some place you've worked. A job position opened. People inside the company knew a about it. Someone said, "Hey, I know a person who would be perfect for the role." Before you knew it, or more precisely, before anyone *outside* the company knew it, the position was filled! No public advertising, no long process of reading multiple résumés and interview lines of candidates. Just a matter of someone finding a job through their inside connections!

That's the hidden job market. The best jobs are never advertised. The positions are filled before there is any need to publish the job opening!

Wouldn't you like to tap into the hidden job market? You really cannot afford to neglect this massive source of great jobs!

There are two primary strategies for finding and fishing in the hidden job market:

- Networking
- Targeting companies

The Importance of Networking

The best bait to get a bite from the hidden job market is a personal referral. HR professionals and hiring managers tend to prefer hiring a candidate that has been referred to them by someone who works at the company. I don't know all the reasons why, but couldn't we describe that as simply human nature?

After all, one of the most basic concerns any hiring authority has about a job candidate is, "Will this person fit in here?" There's probably a natural (if not completely logical) assumption that if a person who works here recommends you, then you will most likely fit in. Regardless of the reason, it is a fact that hiring authorities do tend to prefer candidates who have been referred, especially if the referrer is a current employee.

The importance of networking in all aspects of your job search cannot be overemphasized, particularly in a bad economy. (It's a little easier to find openings in a good economy but in a bad one, you *really* need access to the hidden job market!) Your network can do all the following for you:

- Help you locate hidden job openings
- Introduce you to hiring authorities
- Recommend you to hiring authorities
- Provide important information about the internal workings of the company

Networking is a key strategy in the modern job search. Learn as much as you can about how to network and you will be rewarded with a better job.

Top 10 Job Lead Strategies

Finally, here are my Top 10 Strategies for locating a maximum number of job openings.

1. Set up at least one e-mail job search agent on a general **job search engine** such as www.indeed.com and/or check the job search engine regularly. Also, perform regular searches through specialty job boards such as www.dice.com for persons in the IT specialty.

2. Post a résumé on a general **job boards** such as www.monster.com. Post a résumé on other specialty job boards as appropriate – again, such as www.dice.com for IT professionals.

3. Use the Yellow Pages online, a Chamber of Commerce Directory or another similar source and **target about 25 or 30 companies** that interest you as potential employers. Take the following steps:

    a. Research the company, the names of the HR manager and use your www.linkedin.com account to uncover any other potential contacts in that company.

    b. Send the HR Director or potential hiring manager your résumé with a cover letter. Also, post your résumé to the company's website. Use an ASCII version of your résumé for that purpose. Remember that Applicant Tracking Systems make it possible that the company will search previously submitted résumé if an opening comes available.

    c. About seven days after mailing, follow-up with a phone call to the person you addressed in your cover letter. Do your homework! *Never* address a letter "to whom it may concern". A simple phone call to the company should turn up the appropriate name!

    d. Follow-up with any other contacts you have inside the company.

4. Write a list of all your professional and personal contacts - everyone who could possibly know someone who might provide a job lead. Begin systematically **networking**, calling everyone on the list, letting them know you are looking for a job, and asking them if they know someone who could help you find the kind of job that you want. Repeat every three to six weeks.

5. Prior to beginning your networking efforts in earnest, write out you "**power greeting**" (sometimes called a laser speech or an elevator speech) and memorize it for use in serendipity networking. At a ball game, social event, church function or anywhere else you have an opportunity to do some networking, you will already have in mind exactly what you want to say to a potential contact or networking source.

The speech should be about three sentences in length, stating in a nutshell (a) what your background has been, (b) what your strengths and skills are and (c) what your chief accomplishment(s) have been.

6. Regularly check any newsletters and websites of any **professional organizations** to which you belong. Sometimes job leads will be posted there. Renew membership if necessary.

7. Consider working with **recruiters and employment agencies**. Learn more online and from this book about recruiters and how they work. Determine if working with a recruiter is for you. Get in touch with them.

8. Participate in any **job fairs** in your vicinity. Of course, take your résumé, networking cards and be prepared with your power greeting.

9. Consider using some of your free time for **volunteerism** - for several reasons. It should go without saying that you should only volunteer for a cause you actually believe in, whether it was Habitat for Humanity, a hospital, a church / temple / synagogue, a civic organization or whatever. However, you also want to be doing something that utilizes your skills and if possible where you will meet people. Besides, according to www.careerbuilder.com, 81 percent of employers view volunteering as relevant work experience.

10. Finally, **network extensively**. Yes, I know I already said this two or three times – and yes, it is that important.

7

Stand Out From the Crowd

The term personal branding isn't about self-improvement – it's about self-packaging!

Business guru Tom Peters coined the phrase in 1997 as a part of his forward thinking (at that time) about the ever increasing role each individual will have (and does have!) in a modern economy to add value to a company. His basic line of thought was simple: computers will take over rote activities. People will increasingly be valued for their creative and unique contributions.

The pace of change will decrease the lifespans of job positions. Career and job changes will occur more frequently. Individuals will therefore be forced to clearly define and articulate to potential employers exactly what it is they can contribute. In effect, you become a corporation of one, a brand – marketing your services, skills, strengths and expertise.

That's probably all true but Bob, a 30 year old searching for a sales job, put the same idea in simpler words: "I've been submitting a lot of résumés but it's hard to stand out from the crowd."

Standing out from the crowd is essential and requires skills. That's what this chapter is about.

Understand Your Value Proposition

One very powerful and important strategy for any job seeker is to determine his or her value proposition and find ways to communicate it to each potential employer. In a moment, I will describe what value proposition means.

First though, let me point out that this strategy is especially important to anyone who feels they have an obstacle to overcome in landing the job they want. Here are some real-life obstacles to employment that I have heard from clients over the past several years:

- "I have a gap in my employment history."

- "I was fired from my last job."

- "I am too old."

- "I am too young and inexperienced. How am I supposed to get experience if they won't give me a chance?"

- "I don't have a college degree and although it is not necessary for the job I want, everybody requires a degree."

- "I am overweight and employers hold that against me."

What is a person to do in the light of these very real obstacles? (Whether it is legal or illegal to discriminate against people on the basis of the above items is another question, of course.) There are some specific tactics that apply to each situation. For example, there are ways to de-age a résumé.

However, the one strategy that applies to all these situations is to develop your value proposition and find ways to communicate it. Your value proposition consists of the unique skills and strengths that would benefit an employer – whatever it is that would make you a desirable employee.

Simply put, overcome the disadvantage by demonstrating a convincing case that you are bringing some unique skills and strengths to the table!

For example, an older person may describe her value proposition this way: "I am a mature person who will always show up for work on time." Another worker may describe his value proposition this way: "I am very energetic and creative and bring a lot of enthusiasm to my work." Someone else may say, "I am very experienced and skilled at the tasks this job requires."

The point is, in order to compete in the job marketplace and put your best foot forward, it is important not to become overly discouraged or defensive. Instead, focus on your unique strengths and skills and use every opportunity – cover letters, résumés, interviewing and thank you notes to consistently communicate your personal value proposition to each potential employer.

Does this strategy guarantee that you will land any particular interview and get you a specific job? No. However, overall, it is the best strategy to follow and in my experience will ultimately get results.

You really need to write out a sentence that summarizes your value proposition. Memorize and use it in interviews. State it in the professional summary of your résumé. Support it with facts and in S.T.A.R. stories that illustrate it. Use every interview question as an opportunity to return to your value proposition – this is what I can do for your company!

Seven Strategies for Creating Your Brand / Standing Out from the Crowd

1. Identify your strengths.

2. List your skills.

3. Write down your accomplishments.

4. Write a personal mission statement.

5. Write a laser speech.

6. Write a value proposition.

7. Tailor your résumé and cover letters to reinforce your value proposition.

8

Create an Outstanding Résumé

Here are actual résumé bloopers that I ran across:

- "Hope to hear from you shorty."

- "Have a keen eye for derail."

- "Dear Sir or Madman."

- "I'm attacking my résumé for you to review."

- "I am a rabid typist."

- "My work ethics are impeachable."

- "Nervous of steel."

- "Following is a grief overview of my skills."

- "GPA: 34.0"

Your résumé probably doesn't contain any hilarious bloopers. Come to think of it though, no blooper in your résumé is hilarious. Trust me – your first step in standing out is an outstanding résumé!

Let's start with résumé basics. Sure, there are lots of little tricks to spit polish a résumé but there's no need to go there until all the basics are in place!

Top 10 Basic Rules of Résumés

The primary purpose of a résumé is to get you interviews. The hiring authority reading your résumé will probably look at if *for less than one minute!* I once told a candidate that readers spend 45 seconds or less reading his résumé. He came back to me and said, "I shared your 45-second rule with a recruiter. The recruiter laughed at me and said, 'That's ridiculous – I spend about 15 seconds on one!'"

The point is that you have a few seconds to communicate your value proposition to a potential manager. Here are my 10 basic rules for creating a résumé that will make your phone ring with interview offers.

Rule #1: Tailor the résumé to **address a specific position** and concisely state your unique qualifications for it.

Rule #2: Describe your **most relevant qualifications first**, at the top of the page. New graduates should list educational credentials at the top of the page if they have no other strong qualifications for a position.

Rule #3: **Tailor the résumé to the targeted position**. Use wording common for the industry or profession and list skills and strengths that apply to the job.

Rule #4: **Demonstrate accomplishments** – quantify using numbers, dollars and percentages to illustrate the value you added to the previous employer's business.

Rule #5: **Be concise.** Use bulleted statements. Begin statements with action verbs. Avoid long blocks of text.

Rule #6: **Use the appropriate format.** Typically, this is a chronological résumé. In some cases, if you are changing career fields, a functional résumé may be appropriate.

Even then, you would likely want to use a combination of the chronological and functional formats.

Rule #7: **Create a paper résumé and an ASCII résumé for cutting and pasting into website applications and online profiles.** An ASCII version is a non-formatted version. It's useful because the formatting of a Word document, for example, may not look right when cut and pasted into an online form.

Rule #8: Don't be the guy who wrote, **"have a keen eye for derail"** in his résumé! Proofread the résumé once for spelling and again to check factual statements (phone number, address, dates of employment) and yet again just to make sure it sounds good. Then have someone else proofread it, too!

Rule #9: **Ask a recruiter, human resources manager or hiring manager to read your résumé and provide constructive criticism.** However, keep in mind that if you ask 10 people a question about résumés you will get 10 different answers. Still, it's good to get the perspective of other people with relevant experience or knowledge.

Rule #10: **Print the résumé on plain white paper.** Your résumé is likely to be copied, faxed, and scanned and white paper will reproduce the best copies. Besides, it's just the easiest way to go. If you feel the need to stand out in terms of the color of the paper, a light beige tint is probably your only advisable option. The best way to stand out is to have outstanding content!

3 Strategies for Improving Your Résumé

1. The most fundamental strategy for improving your résumé is to proofread it for grammatical, spelling and factual accuracy.

2. Get feedback on your résumé from recruiters and managers who have hiring authority.

3. Buy and use the best résumé writing guide available, such as Susan Britton Whitcomb's *Résumé Magic: Trade Secrets of a Professional Résumé Writer.*

Résumé Killers?

Occasionally, I'm asked if there are certain overused phrases that are résumé killers. Career consultants differ on the subject but author Liz Ryan expresses the view that there are résumé killer phrases. She says...[vii]

Here are the worst 10 boilerplate phrases -- the ones to seek out and destroy in your résumé as soon as possible:
- Results-oriented professional
- Cross-functional teams
- More than [x] years of progressively responsible experience
- Superior (or excellent) communication skills
- Strong work ethic
- Met or exceeded expectations
- Proven track record of success
- Works well with all levels of staff
- Team player
- Bottom-line orientation

My view is that there are situations in which it is better to use alternative approaches to a traditional résumé. There may be job positions, industries, corporate cultures and areas of the country that value innovation and creativity over conservative traditions. However, I would no more advise every client of mine to write a creative, free-wheeling résumé any more than I would advise everyone to feel free to wear blue jeans and a sweatshirt to an interview.

Sure, in some cases it might work and may even help you but in many cases, a dark suit is still your best bet!

As for the boilerplate phrases in the article above, remember the average résumé passes through at least one software program for keyword scanning before reaching a pair of human eyes. Potential employers will not search for creative wording during the scanning process; they will scan for the traditional wording that matches the job responsibilities and requirements. So don't let "creativity" weed you out of the running on the first round!

"Well," you may say, "I'm not so concerned about how a computer program reads my résumé. I'm concerned about the humans who will be reading it." Good point! So bear in mind that the average recruiter or hiring manager spends *less than one minute* with a résumé the first time they look at it.

Frankly, they scan it. They are looking for some basic information quickly. It definitely may be to your advantage to present a résumé that follows a conventional format and uses the kind of terms the reader is expecting.

The most up-to-date technique is individualization. Approach your résumé as an opportunity to find a unique approach to presenting your experiences, strengths and skills in a way most appropriate for your personality, industry and situation.

How to De-Age Your Résumé

Your résumé is not a biography. In fact, it's not necessarily a complete accounting of every job you ever held. It is a synopsis of relevant information about your experiences, skills, strengths and accomplishments sufficient to indicate whether a prospective employer should go to the trouble of interviewing you.

Therefore, it is usually not necessary to include information about jobs you held more than 10 years ago. In fact, information more than 10 years old is almost by definition irrelevant and outdated.

If you are a younger worker, then this issue is not a problem for you, of course. However, if you are an older worker, this issue is relevant to you and it presents an opportunity to de-age your résumé. As I have mentioned before, age discrimination in hiring is illegal, but it happens.

De-aging your résumé won't completely solve the problem but it may get you in the door for an interview and once there you have a fair shot at presenting yourself and your unique value proposition in the best possible light. So here's how to de-age your résumé:

- You may not want to include an exact number of years of experience in your professional summary. Instead of saying this:

  "32 years of experience…"

  You may want to say this:

  "More than 25 years of experience"

- Don't go back more than 10 years in the professional experience section of your résumé. Anything older than that you can just leave off. (Of course, if you have been at the XYZ Company for the past 32 years, then you can't leave that off.)

- Don't put dates with your education or degrees.

Finally, de-aging your résumé isn't the only strategy you need to overcome potential age discrimination. You also should consider the following:

- Update your wardrobe and hairstyle. I'm not saying that a 55 year old should try to look 25 years old again… but do present a *youthful* 55 appearance.

- Be energetic in your speech and presentation of yourself. Don't come across as tired and worn out.

- Focus on your value proposition: the experiences, skills, strengths and accomplishments that make you unique.

- If it seems appropriate, point out the advantages of an experienced worker: dependability and well… experience!

- Counter common misconceptions of mature people. State that you are open-minded, continually learning, fun to work with and innovative.

Need a Résumé Writer?

Résumé writing rip-offs exist out there in the market. However, with your future on the line, a great résumé can be worth its weight in gold. I write résumés – very good ones – but the best and most passionate résumé writer I know is Ginger Korljan at www.TakeChargeCoaching.com. Tell her I sent you!

Résumé: a written exaggeration of only the good things a person has done in the past, as well as a wish list of the qualities a person would like to have.

~Bo Bennett~

9

Use a Variety of Strategies to Get Job Leads

A major part of your job search effort is to find job openings. Here is what I recommend in order to find the maximum number of opportunities.

More than One Way to Skin a Cat

There's more than one way to find job openings and you need to use them all.

I have seen studies based on inside information from the outplacement industry. One aspect of those studies is to determine how the participants originally learned about the jobs they subsequently landed. Here are the current facts:[viii]

Networking is the number one way that people learn about job openings that actually lead to employment. You cannot over-estimate the importance of networking in your job search! You need networking for many aspects of a job search:
- To locate openings
- To learn names of important contacts
- To get internal recommendations
- To collect inside information on a company's culture and hiring practices

Published openings (primarily on the Internet) account for a large percentage of the opportunities that lead to jobs. However, there is significantly more effectiveness of published openings for jobs with salaries under $60k. The bigger the job, the more important the networking!

Recruiters are the third most effective way of locating job openings that will lead to actual employment. Incidentally, one of my candidates just reported that his recruiter told him, "The first thing I do after getting a résumé is check out the person's profile on LinkedIn.com. You can read more about LinkedIn and why you may want to use it in Chapter 10.

Some people do get jobs by **posting a résumé online**. However, if all you are doing is posting a résumé online, you may be waiting on a job for a very long time!

What do these facts suggest for job search strategy? In short, I recommend a mix of strategies. It is vital to search the Internet, post your résumé and be present in online networking sites such as LinkedIn.com. However, Internet strategies should be blended with networking for it is also vital to continuously expand and utilize your network of contacts in terms of both locating opportunities and actually landing the job.

12 Strategies for Locating Job Leads

1. Make a list of all your professional and personal contacts - everyone who could possibly know someone in a position to provide a job lead. Begin systematically calling everyone on your list and renew your acquaintance with them. Let them know that you are looking for a job and ask them if they know anyone who could help you. Then call those people, introduce yourself, and ask them for any advice they may have about finding a job.

2. Don't forget to network online! Set up a www.linkedin.com profile. Explore the possibilities of using www.facebook.com or www.twitter.com for networking purposes, too.

3. Regularly search the major internet job boards such as Monster, Hot Jobs and Career Builder. However, don't forget

the more targeted niche job boards, such as Dice for the IT professionals or local job boards.

4. Post your résumé on those job boards. Also, every two weeks go back to each posted résumé and make a very small modification. (Each time you modify the résumé it will show up on the site as a new posting.)

5. Use the Internet or the Yellow Pages and target about 25 to 30 companies where you might enjoy working. Begin by (a) researching them, finding out the name of the HR Manager as well as any other person in your personal or professional network who works there; (b) mailing your résumé with a great cover letter and / or post your résumé on their website; (c) following up about seven days after mailing with a phone call to the HR Manager. Of course, if you have a personal or professional contact inside the company, call that person and ask them to introduce you.

6. Write out your power greeting or laser speech and memorize it. That way, you are prepared at any time to do some networking. You can find resources on the Internet that will help you write your power greeting. By the way, your power greeting can also be modified into your best answer to the standard interview question, "Tell me a little about yourself."

7. Regularly check any newsletters and websites of professional organizations to which you belong. Sometimes job leads will be posted there.

8. Consider using some of your free time to volunteer. We discussed reasons earlier in the book.

9. Consider working with recruiters and employment agencies. Determine if working with those resources is for you and if it is, get in touch with them.

10. Participate in job fairs. Of course, take copies of your résumé, networking cards and be prepared with your power greeting.

11. A relatively new way of searching for job leads is through job match websites, such as www.jobfox.com or www.unitedwework.com. You can post profile information and be matched to current job listings.

12. Say your prayers and have faith. Whether they call it divine providence or simple serendipity, people with positive, hopeful attitudes seem to attract job openings!

Are Job Fairs Worth Your Time?

Jack e-mailed me.

> "I got a job! It was through a job fair two weeks ago. Things moved pretty fast, but I was accepted. Now I'm sorting out all the paperwork they gave me and tying up loose ends here before I start. The pay is only fair but the benefits are pretty good. In this economy any decent job is very good!"

He went from job fair to job candidate to new hire in a little over two weeks. Not bad, especially since I originally had to talk him into going to the job fair in the first place. I can understand his reluctance. When he had stopped by a job fair once before, he found it crowded, chaotic and confusing. (Not that all job fairs are like that, but the one Jack attended was that way.)

So, he didn't want to go back. Why waste the time?

The reason, as I had earlier explained to Jack, is you can't afford to leave any stone unturned in a serious job search.

After reading his e-mail, I called and asked Jack about his experience with his job search and what he would like to pass along to my other clients. After all, he's getting to be quite an expert. He and his wife combined have eight job transitions over the past several years!

Jack said, "I don't think there is a magic bullet for the job search. You have to do it all – post your résumé, use the Internet job search engines, connect with agencies and recruiters, constantly network and yes, attend the job fairs."

I agree… and that's the major point of this section of the book. Use all available strategies – and even Jack's list does not include all of them!

So, watch for local job fairs and attend them. When you go, take fresh copies of your résumé and some nice networking or business cards. Prepare your laser presentation. Talk to anyone and everyone there. You may be glad you did!

Your income is a direct reward for the quality and quantity of the services you render to your world. Whatever field you are in, if you want to double your income, you simply have to double the quality and quantity of what you do for that income. Or you have to change activities and occupations so that what you are doing is worth twice as much.

~Brian Tracy~

10

Network, Network, Network... and Did I Mention Networking?

Scott was blasting résumés with absolutely no results except for an increasing level of frustration. However, he was very open to suggestions.

Although he really thought his résumé was good like it was, I convinced him to let me help him tweak it a little. Then, based on coaching and the dismal results he was experiencing, he dropped the résumé blasting and began networking in earnest.

In a matter of about six weeks, Scott called and told me he had landed a great new job. I asked him if he had any advice for my other candidates and he sent me the e-mail below.

> Bud:
>
> I cannot stress enough the power of networking in any job search. Having been displaced and in need of finding a new job, I found that networking was the most effective way to uncover true job openings and networking was the best way to get an actual response on any potential opportunity. Blindly sending résumés to organizations or posts on the internet got me nowhere. It was networking that led me to my new opportunity and new company. Build a strong network and stay in touch with the people in the network you build!
>
> -Scott

Scott's words echo the same message hundreds of my job search clients over the years have repeated to me time after time – networking makes a difference.

Don't Waste Your Time Looking for a Job

The fact is, if you are spending all your time looking for a job in the newspaper or on the Internet, you are wasting your time!

I speak with dozens of job-seekers across the country each week, many of whom are either finding jobs or are currently in the process of getting interviews. Others are not nearly as successful and here's the difference. From my vantage point, it is as clear as crystal.

The people looking in the newspaper and on the Internet are finding nothing except for scams and lower level sales work.

Then there are those like my client Evan who stopped looking for a job and started looking for connections!

Evan and I spoke one morning during our regularly scheduled call. He was very excited!

In the past couple of weeks he made it down to the final interview stage with one company and was expecting to hear their final decision on the day of our call. In addition, he had also landed phone interviews over the next few weeks with a couple more great companies.

He said, "Bud, it has all been through networking. Prior to talking with you I sent out scores of résumés and got NO responses. After talking with you about networking, I pulled out all the stops, set up my Linkedin profile and started talking to everyone I could find."

"I am very confident I will land a job soon, and every opportunity has come to me through networking!"

So the main lesson about searching for a job today is – don't! Focus on renewing connections and making contacts. Have your laser speech ready and a well-written résumé on hand to pass along.

Get busy on LinkedIn and on the phone.

Your 15-second Elevator Pitch

Your elevator pitch (aka laser speech) is a concise explanation of your job search that can help you network more effectively and confidently. A great website to help you put together your elevator pitch is www.15secondpitch.com.

The method used on 15secondpitch.com isn't the only way to put together an elevator pitch but it's a good tool to make sure you keep it short and sweet. It allows you to enter 500 characters and asks:

* Your name
* Your profession
* Specialization
* What you do
* Why you're the best
* Your call to action

You can enter an e-mail and password for the elevator pitch to be sent to you via e-mail (or you can just copy and paste it into a Word document).

Networking is No Laughing Matter

My client Kyle left an excited voicemail for me, "Bud, you don't need to call me anymore. I've found a job!"

Despite Kyle's statement, I called him immediately.

"Hi, Kyle, congratulations! How did you land the job?"

Kyle's answer was no surprise to me all. In fact, it was predictable.

"Well," said Kyle, "The day I got laid off, I called a friend that I used to work for. He got laid off before I did and went to work for another company. So I called him up and said jokingly, 'Have you got a job for me? I just got laid off!'" To make a long story short, he actually said there was a possibility and arranged for me to come in for some interviews and I got the job!"

Why am I not surprised? Surely by now you've gotten the point but in case you haven't, networking is still the number one source of job leads that eventually lead to employment.

Networking helped Kyle land a job within three months of being laid off. Even though he jokingly called his friend, networking in the job search is no joking matter!

LinkedIn

One of the options you may want to consider in terms of maximizing your online presence is the professional networking website LinkedIn.com. You probably are familiar with at least the name because many thousands of professionals are now using it to help maintain their professional network. Plus, it is a source of some job leads that are sometimes published nowhere else.

Other Social Media and Networking

Don't forget social media as opportunities for networking. For example, use Facebook.com to reconnect with friends.

Also, there are other ways of networking, such as job seeker national networking organizations like Pinkslipmixers.com.

The Plant Lady

Lisa asked me if I wanted to hear a funny story.

I said, "Sure."

She said, "You know that interview I just had with that awesome company? I got that interview because of the plant lady."

"I beg your pardon," I replied.

"Yes, the plant lady. She is the lady at my former place of employment who used to come around and water the plants. Well, she does the same for the other company, too."

"Well, I used to speak to the plant lady every week when she would come into water the plants. When I got laid off, she knew it. Somehow she heard of this opening at the other company and immediately thought of me."

"When she came into my old company this week to water the plants she told the receptionist that she had heard of a great job for me. So she and the receptionist called me and I got the interview. Isn't that funny?" Lisa asked, smiling.

What do you think about this true story?

Of course, there's the obvious connection about networking – but really this story is about something bigger than that. Lisa didn't get this opportunity because she was networking with the plant lady; she got this opportunity because she took the time to speak with the plant lady from week to week.

It illustrates for me a great principle for success in your life – the person that you encounter at any given moment is the most important person in your life at that given moment. So if that person is the plant lady, take time to speak with her.

You never know where any particular relationship will lead or what blessings may unfold for you at a later time.

Years ago, I was in charge of providing hospitality to some of the invited speakers at a church convention. I didn't know some of the people and was trying to spot them in a crowd.

I turned to a clergyman and friend of mine, pointed to someone in the crowd and said, "Sam, is that person a VIP?"

Sam looked at me for a moment and said, "Bud, everyone is a VIP."

So, remember the plant lady and later on she just may take care of you.

11

Shine Like a Star in the Interview

You must prepare for interviews and this chapter will help you do that. Key aspects include:

- Select the appropriate clothes to wear
- Consider your grooming and style
- Write out your value proposition
- Prepare and practice answers to common questions
- Prepare and practice answers to difficult questions
- Research the company and utilize your network
- Determine the fair market value of the position you are seeking
- Brush up on negotiating tactics
- Think thoughts that will generate positive energy

By the way, don't make the mistake of taking phone screen type interviews for granted. You need to prepare for phone screens, too!

The Phone Interview is Not a "Gimme"!

The phone interview – an initial screening interview over the phone, often with a lower level Human Resources employee – used to be considered a "gimme". No longer!

Here's a perspective from the Wall Street Journal:

> Job seekers, beware the telephone.
>
> For years, the phone interview was a preliminary step that allowed an employer to give a candidate the once-over and schedule an in-person interview. But these days,

many recruiters are using the phone interview to pose the kinds of in-depth questions previously reserved for finalists. What's more, job hunters say the bar for getting to the next level has been raised much higher, catching many of them off-guard.

In a recent first interview for a senior marketing job, Robyn Cobb was grilled by a hiring manager for an hour and a half on topics ranging from her work history and marketing philosophy to her knowledge of the company and its industry.

"I thought it was never going to end," says the 45-year-old Ms. Cobb, who lives in Alpharetta, Ga., and was laid off in December from a midsize communications firm.

Until recently, candidates could often breeze through most phone interviews in 10 minutes or less by answering a few softball questions. Little preparation was necessary, and most people could expect to be invited for a "real" interview before hanging up.

These days, job hunters are finding that they need to reserve an hour or more for a phone interview. They may be asked to discuss their full work history, including the exact dates of their experience in various business areas. They may also be expected to cite examples and exact stats that illustrate their strengths and offer details on how they would handle the position.[ix]

How do you prepare for a phone screen interview? Just as you would for a face-to-face interview.

The only difference? You don't have to worry about how to dress. However, you do have to remind yourself of good phone etiquette! Make sure you are in a quiet room – no barking dogs, no kids crying in the background and no leaving the caller "for just a moment while I go answer the doorbell!"

Dress for Interviewing Success

Much has been written about proper attire for interviews. The basic rules for a professional look are simple:

Women's Interview Attire
- Solid color, conservative suit
- Coordinated blouse
- Moderate shoes
- Limited jewelry
- Neat, professional hairstyle
- Tan or light hosiery
- Sparse make-up
- Manicured nails

Men's Interview Attire
- Solid color, conservative suit
- White long sleeve shirt
- Conservative tie
- Dark socks, professional shoes
- Very limited jewelry
- Neat, professional hairstyle
- Neatly trimmed nails

No, it's not necessary to wear a suit for some positions and industries. My rule of thumb is to dress one level above what normal day-to-day wear in the office would be normally. If normal wear for the position is jeans and golf shirt, then at a minimum, wear business casual to the interview. When in doubt, it's always better to overdress than to underdress.

Finally, go very easy on the perfume or aftershave. Frankly, when it comes to odor, you never know what someone else likes, so you don't want to leave one – good or bad.

Interview Types, Styles and Formats

There are numerous types, styles and formats for interviews. Some of the concepts overlap. You can prepare yourself for interviewing by understanding these potential scenarios.

- Informal – some companies have no structured way in which they interview and some interviewers simply engage potential employees in off-the-cuff conversations. This is rare, especially in larger companies, but you may encounter an interview like this in a smaller company or at the hands of an inexperienced hiring manager.

- Formal – some companies standardize their hiring processes, take a structured approach, and train their managers and recruiters how to select new employees more objectively.

- Phone Screen – typically, this is a short phone conversation with a lower-level employee whose purpose is to weed out unqualified candidates. However, in difficult economic times, phone interviews tend to become more lengthy and rigorous, so take them seriously!

- Single Interviewer – you may speak with one person only throughout the entire hiring process.

- Multiple Interviewers in Sequence – you may speak with several different persons over a period of time through the hiring process, representing different aspects of the company, to include:

1. The hiring manager, your potential boss
2. The HR manager or other HR representative
3. A higher level authority such as your potential boss's boss
4. A peer-level person (this person's mission typically is to help determine if you will fit in)
5. A subject matter expert to help determine if you know the right stuff

Sometimes, you will be asked to meet with a number of different people over the course of one day. Usually, the company will provide an agenda so you will know to whom you will be speaking.

- Panel Interview – this interview also consists of multiple interviewers but in this case, they all meet with you at the same time.

- Traditional Interview – a broad-based conversation between one interviewer and a job candidate using behavioral style questions ("tell me about yourself", "what are your strengths and weaknesses", "what would you do if…", etc…).

  Some interviewers may also pose technical questions to probe an applicant's expertise. Your strategy in this type of interview is to build a rapport with the interviewer and demonstrate opinions and information that will cause the interviewer to view you as competent.

- Competency-based Interview – usually for lower level positions in which the interviewer is simply trying to determine if the candidate can and will do the job.

  May involve questions that ask for examples to provide evidence of a skill, ability or trait ("tell me about a time that you....""). Your strategy in this type of interview is to be well-prepared with S.T.A.R. stories!

- Performance-based Behavioral Interview – often used for mid-level or higher positions; similar to a competency-based interview but more extensive. You will be asked multiple questions about past history, activities and achievements, with multiple opportunities to give examples of what you achieved and how you achieved it.

  Your strategy is to be extremely well-versed and practiced at outlining your career experiences, skills, attributes and accomplishments – and to be prepared to support all with several S.T.A.R. stories!

Less frequently encountered types of interview include:

- Situational Interview (also called problem solving interview or scenario-based interview) – the interviewer provides a hypothetical situation and the candidate is asked to solve it. You will be evaluated by how well you solve the problem within a time limit. You may encounter a situation in which you are asked to actually work with other candidates to solve a problem. The purpose is to assess your team-working skills and style. Generally, you would only encounter this kind of interview in a very complex and thorough hiring process.

- Stress Interview – the title of which begs the question, "Are there any interviews that are *not* stressful?" Maybe not, but there are some interviews *designed* to be extremely stressful!

  The interviewers may set you up with such tactics as letting you wait a long time before beginning the interview, treating you rudely or allowing some kind of disruptive events during the interview. Obviously, it's all designed to assess how you react to pressure. Stress interviews are not common but they aren't unheard of, so your strategy (as in any interview) is to stay cool, calm and collected.

- Flash Interview – a quick meeting with a senior executive to give a candidate a final approval. If you are invited to meet a senior executive, even if only briefly, it's a good sign! Your strategy is to listen, answer any questions succinctly, and be prepared to ask a couple of intelligent, informed questions about the executive's vision for the company and how your position will support it.

Overcoming Nervousness

Greg secured his first interview in more than 20 years! Recently laid off, he had hustled and within weeks found an opportunity. The interview was a week away and we were preparing for it. I asked Greg what he thought his biggest need was in terms of getting ready.

Without hesitating, he said, "Controlling my nerves!"

Like lots of people, Greg found the thought of interviewing rather stressful. It's no wonder, really.

1. He hadn't interviewed in 20 years and didn't know what to expect.

2. He really wanted the job so there was a lot on the line.

3. The fact is that people do lose opportunities because of poor interviewing skills.

So, I gave Greg some tips for calming his nerves on the day of the interview. Maybe these will help you, too!

1. Monitor your self-talk. Don't say things like, "They probably won't like me!" Focus on the positive, "I have a lot to offer".

2. Just prior to entering the building and the room of the interview, use a public speaker's trick and take a couple of deep breaths.

3. Give yourself permission to forget something. If you are asked a question and your mind goes blank, don't panic. Just say, "You know, that's a good question but I can't seem to think of an answer right now. May we come back to it later?" Almost any interviewer will say, "Sure!"

4. Prepare well, but just relax and be yourself once the interview begins.

5. Remember, the interviewer is just another person trying to do his or her job.

Keys to Answering Interview Questions

The first key to answering interview questions is keep one thing in mind: your primary goal in answering interviewing questions is to convey to the potential employer your skills, experiences and strengths. After all, from the employer's perspective, the point is to find a person who has the right set of skills and will fit in well.

Let me give an example of how this principle works. Elaine, one of my clients, asked how to answer this question: "Why do you want this job?"

My reply was that her answer should be designed to once again emphasize the skills, experiences and strengths she would bring to the table. Here are a couple of sample answers to illustrate what I meant.

"This job is a great opportunity and this company is a place where my qualifications can make a difference. As a customer service professional well versed in all aspects of call centers, I see this position as perfect for me. There will be enough challenge to keep me on my toes. That's the kind of job I can look forward to every day. "

"I want this job because it seems tailor-made for the kind of things I do well, which include customer service and communicating with all kinds of people. As I said earlier, in a previous position I was given a customer service award and this seems to be a place where I could use those skills."

"I'd fit right in as a receptionist in your firm. I have observed that the receptionist position requires competence at handling several activities in quick order -- customer service, answering the phone and filing papers. I like multitasking and in my previous jobs I have a lot of practice in keeping all the balls in the air."

"I understand that this is a growing company. Your website says you are launching new products and expanding. I want be a part of this business as it grows. I believe my unique set of skills could really make a contribution."

You have other objectives in an interview besides answering questions, such as establishing rapport with the interviewer and finding out as much information as you can about the company, the hiring process, the compensation and the job. However, remember the following.

Your objective in answering interview questions is to convey to the potential employer your skills, experiences and strengths. Massage that information into every answer!

Now you know your objective in answering interview questions, the concept of S.T.A.R. stories can often provide the best method for answering those questions!

S.T.A.R. Stories

Behavioral interviewing is a term that describes asking the interviewee questions about past behavior. Most managers and recruiters who have had any kind of instructions about conducting interviews have been trained to ask behavioral questions, such as...

1. Give me an example of a time when you set a goal and were able to meet or achieve it.

2. Tell me about a time when you had to use your presentation skills.

3. Give me a specific example of a time when you had to conform to a policy with which you did not agree.

4. Tell me about a time when you had to go above and beyond the call of duty in order to get a job done.

5. What is your typical way of dealing with conflict? Give me an example.

6. Tell me about a time you were able to successfully deal with another person even when that individual may not have personally liked you (or vice versa).

7. Tell me about a difficult decision you've made in the last year.

8. Tell me about a recent situation in which you had to deal with a very upset customer or co-worker.

9. Give me an example of a time when you motivated others.

The common aspect of all the questions above is this: *they are asking for a real-life example from your previous work experience.* Another common aspect of these questions: answered properly, they will make you shine like a star in the interview! Think about it. What could be better? The interviewer is asking you to tell a story about yourself that will show you in a positive light!

Unfortunately, many interviews go like this:

Interviewer: *So tell me about your typical way of dealing with conflict.*

Jack: *... (pause)... um.... well, of course, I try to avoid conflicts with people as much as I can.... Um.... that's a good question. I guess I just tell it like it is but you know I try to get along with everybody, you know... yeah... so, hmm... that's a good question. Yeah, I guess I handle conflict tactfully and try to get along with everyone.*

Are you impressed? Probably not... Neither is the interviewer! However, the interviewer asks another candidate (who happens to know about S.T.A.R. stories) and the conversation goes like this:

Interviewer: *So tell me about your typical way of dealing with conflict.*

John: *That's a good question... Kind of difficult to answer, because I tend to get along with people well.*

If asked about dealing with conflict, the first thing to do is make sure to point out that you get along with people well and it's hard to think of an example. However, the interviewer may press for an answer and if so, use the S.T.A.R. format, as follows.

John first describes the **S**ituation:

> John (continuing): *I can think of one situation where people in my department – the quality department – were complaining that the supervisors in the production department were not responding quickly to requests to correct processing issues. They felt like the supervisors were basically blowing them off.*

John then describes his **T**ask:

> John (continuing): *So, as the quality manager, the thing I needed to do was to get both sides working together.*

John proceeds to his **A**ctions:

> John (continuing): *I went to the production manager and told him that my people had complained about an issue but I made it clear that I wasn't sure what all the facts were and simply asked him if we could talk about it and see if there were any solutions. He agreed and talked to his supervisors. Turns out, they had some complaints about my people not following certain procedures. So I investigated that and found out that in some cases it wasn't true. Throughout the entire process, I made sure the production manager and I collaborated together. I didn't want to get into some kind of blame game.*

Finally, John wraps up by showing how his actions yielded positive **R**esults:

> John (concludes): *As a result of the collaborative approach I took and my willingness to look at any problems on my end, the production manager and I addressed this conflict and within a week, tensions were down considerably. More important, production was flowing yet quality issues were being addressed in a timely manner. I think that's a good example of how I deal with conflict.*

What do you think? If you were the hiring manager and needed to hire someone who could deal with daily conflicts, who would you hire? Jack or John?

S.T.A.R. stories are a great method for answering interview questions. Properly used, they will make you shine like a STAR in the interview!

Establishing Rapport with the Interviewer

What do hiring managers and recruiters really want to know when they interview a potential job candidate? Usually, they want to know three things:

1. *Can* this person do the job?
2. *Will* this person do the job?
3. How well will this person *fit in?*

Your aim in answering interview questions is to demonstrate that you can do the job and to a lesser extent, that you will do the job. However, convincing the interviewer that you will fit in is far more subjective. (I might add that you also want to be determining if their corporate culture is a good fit for you.)

The first and most important step to communicating that you will fit in is to *establish rapport with the interviewer.* Like all social skills, this may be more of an art than a science. Still, there are skills involved and there are things you can do to help you connect with the interviewer.

By the way, I realize that some job candidates are more extroverted than others, some job candidates are better talkers than others and that some interviewers are easier to warm up to than others. Just being an extrovert doesn't necessarily mean you will do a perfect job of establishing rapport with an interviewer. However, it is in your best interest to give it your best shot, so here are a few suggestions.

1. **Make a good first impression.** Dress and groom appropriately and show up on time. Otherwise, you are definitely starting off in the hole!

2. **Look for common ground.** Pick up on anything that you and the interviewer may have in common: same alma mater, fan of the same team, kids go to the same school, used to work for the same employer – anything to help you connect. The flip side: this is NOT the time to point out differences!

3. **Actively listen.** You generate good vibrations when you pay attention, are alert and listen carefully to the interviewer. You're never going to meet an interviewer who doesn't want to be heard and respected. Practice listening and giving your undivided attention!

4. **Use body language** to communicate enthusiasm and a high level of energy, but with an appropriate degree of restraint. Here are some specifics:

   a. Offer a firm, confident handshake.
   b. Sit up straight, lean slightly forward, face the interviewer directly.
   c. Do not cross your arms.
   d. Look the person in the eye but don't bore through them, glance away from time-to-time.

5. **Mirror the interviewer's body language and verbal statements.** Don't overdo this to the point that it's awkward and strange, of course. However, as a general rule, it creates positive feelings if you mirror the interviewer: if she smiles, you smile. If she seems to be in deep thought, furrow your brow a little, too. Suppose the interviewer spends time explaining the company's current plans to increase efficiency and that efficiency is the current focus. It may be appropriate to respond by saying, "It seems that your company is really focused on improved efficiencies right now."

6. **Ask informed, relevant, intelligent questions**. In school, there are no dumb questions. However, in interview, there may be dumb questions! I am referring to the mistake of not paying attention. Make sure you listen carefully. However, if you listen very carefully but still don't understand a point the interviewer is speaking about, ask for clarification. It will show that you are engaged in the conversation.

7. **Listen carefully**. OK, I already said that. Still, it's important. I once heard a philosopher say that people feel loved when they feel heard. I don't know what you think about that, but I will assure you that if you listen carefully, the interviewer is more likely to feel that you are the type of person they would like around there!

Industrial Espionage

No, we are not really going to discuss industrial espionage here but you do want to learn all you can in the interview. Remember that *you* are interviewing *them* as much as *they* are interviewing *you*. If it makes if more fun, think of an interview as an opportunity to conduct a little industrial espionage. You want to learn the following kinds of valuable information during your interviews.

- The history, health, culture, and future plans of company

- The hiring process: how it works, who else is competing for the same job, where you stand as a candidate, what are the next steps, who is the actual decision-maker and when can you follow-up

- The compensation structure, including all benefits which will be included

- The job: what are the requirements and expectations, how does it relate to the strategic direction of the firm, to whom will you report

How do you go about soliciting this information? First, listen carefully. Secondly, be prepared to ask about those things anytime you are given the opportunity.

Finally, your industrial espionage should begin *before* you ever go to the interview! Research the firm on the Internet. Find out the names of the president/CEO and learn a little about them. Call any connections you have. Research industry standards for compensation. Knowledge is power. Know everything you can before you arrive for the interview!

Common questions

You can't anticipate every interview question, but you can anticipate (and prepare for) many of them! There are very common interview questions. These are important to know because you can prepare your S.T.A.R. stories in advance. I'm not saying to memorize them but do write them out and think through them!

Here are 10 very common interview questions. Some of them can be answered with S.T.A.R. stories and some can not. Below I give a few tips on answering each of them.

1. **Tell me about yourself.** Don't go into personal details. Stick to a brief description of (a) your educational and career background, (2) a few words about your best skills, attributes, strengths and abilities and (3) a short description of one of your best accomplishments.

2. **Why did you leave your last job?** Keep your answer positive, no matter what happened! Never talk bad about any former firm, bosses or fellow employees. If the situation was bad, simply indicate, "I left to look for a better opportunity" or something of that nature.

3. **What did you make in your last position?** It's hard to avoid answering such a direct question (which often is asked in phone screen interviews). If asked in a phone interview, you may be able to answer like this: "I will be glad to discuss personal details like that a little further into the process."

4. **How much salary do you need?** This question is the beginning of a game and the first person to name a number loses! Avoid giving an exact number and instead say something like this: "Good question. My requirements depend on the nature of the job, actually. I am sure you are working with a range. What is your range for this position?"

5. **What are your strengths?** Prepare to answer this with a S.T.A.R. story. "I feel one of my greatest strengths is customer service. For example..." Be ready to name and discuss a couple of additional strengths, if asked.

6. **What is your weakest point?** The oldest advice on the books is to answer this question by naming a trait that could be a strength: "Gee, I guess I work too much." A more sincere but relatively safe answer is to *name an area in which you have greatly improved*. In other words, you are actually indentifying an area that *used to be* a weakness. Use a S.T.A.R. story.

Interviewer: What do you feel is your weakest point?

Paul: Listening to others, perhaps, although I've greatly improved in that area. For example, I was working on a team and certain people pointed out that I wasn't asking for the team members' ideas. I realized this was true and that my task was to get everyone's input. So I started deliberately going to each team member and asking them for their ideas. The results were that we ended up using many of those ideas and the team was very complimentary about my leadership.

So, my natural tendency is sometimes to make a plan and move ahead quickly, but I am learning that it is very important to listen.

7. **Tell me about a time you had a problem or conflict with a supervisor (or a coworker or customer).** Use a S.T.A.R. story to answer this kind of question. Obviously, make sure that the story presents how you *skillfully* handled the situation! It's probably best if you really can't remember having a serious conflict with a supervisor. (If you answer this question in regard to a supervisor, don't use the opportunity to show how right you were! Use it to show how easy you are to get along with!)

8. **Why should I hire you?** This is a golden opportunity to lay out your value proposition once more. Focus on what you bring to the organization: your experiences, skills, strengths, knowledge, attributes and history of accomplishments. Just focus on reiterating those themes.

9. **Where do you see yourself in five years?** Tricky question. Keep your answer generic. Don't suggest you want your boss's job. Don't suggest that the current company is just a stepping stone.

   Say that you want to focus first on making sure you perform your new job with excellence, but that you would hope that in five years you will have proved your ability to handle greater responsibilities and make a larger contribution with the company.

10. **Do you have any questions for me?** Yes, you should have a couple of questions. We discuss appropriate questions elsewhere in this book.

Difficult questions

My client Louis landed a job fairly quickly. Unfortunately, about two months later I received this e-mail from him.

> Hi Bud,
>
> I'm sure you didn't expect to hear from me again, let alone so soon!
>
> (Louis went on to explain that he was back in the job search even though he had not yet quit the new job. He continued…)
>
> My new job is not what I was hoping for at all. I am routinely screamed at, sworn at, insulted and hung up on. The people we get calls from are being cheated left and right by the companies we do the payment processing for and we get all the fallout. It is a real nightmare!
>
> How do I discuss or convey this – or not – as I hopefully get new interviews? I know you're not supposed to say negative things about past employers, but what would be my reasons for leaving a job in this bad economy that I can talk about?
>
> Any help would be appreciated.
>
> Thanks,
> *Louis*

Louis knew that the issue of leaving a job he hated after working there only a couple of months could present an issue in an interview. We discussed the possibility of not including this experience on his résumé which would eliminate the question about leaving a company so quickly. However, in the event that

Louis decided to leave the new bad job on his résumé, I offered this suggestion:

> My advice is as follows:
>
> You should think through a brief explanation of why you are leaving the current position and stick to it without elaboration throughout interviews.
>
> "Yes, I know it is strange to leave a position so soon, especially in this economy. Normally, I wouldn't think of it. The job turned out to be very different from what I expected. After a lot of soul-searching, I decided the best thing for me to do would simply be to continue my job search."
>
> If pressed for more info, you can say something of this nature:
>
> "You know, I feel a certain amount of loyalty to my current employer despite the fact that I strongly disagree with some of their practices. So I prefer to simply leave it at this: I don't feel comfortable with some of the things I have been asked to do there and would prefer to find other employment."
>
> *Bud*

There are difficult questions for which there are not perfect answers. Here's another situation that can generate difficult questions and strategies for answering them.

Situation:
There is a gap in your work history. The interviewer asks why.

Answer:
Your answer will depend partly on the reason for the gap.

However, as I stated in Chapter 1, remember that when the interviewer asks you about the gap in your work history, they probably have a deeper concern that they aren't stating. What the interviewer is *really* worried about is something like this:

- Were you in prison, drug or alcohol rehabilitation or recuperating from a serious illness?
- Are you a lazy person who simply took a long vacation?
- Is there something so bad about you that you couldn't land a job?

Listen carefully and try to discern the real concern. Tailor your answer to (a) give a brief, factual reason for the gap and (b) address the deeper concern.

Example:

> Interviewer: *I notice that there is a gap in your work history from 2004 – 2005. Why is that?*
>
> Lois: *Yes, I left the ABC Company in early 2004 due to a major reorganization. My entire department was eliminated. My father passed away just before that and my mother had to have serious surgery just afterward. So I delayed my job search for about six months while I was taking care of Mom.*
>
> *However, she recuperated and I was eager to get back to work. So I landed my next job in January of 2005. It was a necessary but temporary change in my plans. However, I am dedicated to my career and am very eager to dedicate myself to working for a growing firm like yours!*

You can use the same principles to deal with some of the most difficult questions. Give a brief, factual explanation and provide assurances that will address underlying concerns. You may not always convince an interviewer but you will have done the best possible: an honest, defensible answer.

Use the Interview to Set-up Your Negotiating Position Properly or... The First Person to Name a Number Loses

One of the things you do NOT want to do in an interview is make statements that will complicate or compromise your ability to negotiate the best possible compensation later down the line. Here are some danger zones and tips on navigating through them.

Danger Zone #1: You may be asked, "What did you earn in your last position?" There are two dangers here. The first is that the hiring firm may disqualify you on the basis of being too expensive, assuming you will not take a lower amount and that if you did, you would be dissatisfied and leave as soon as possible. The second danger is that the firm will make an offer based on your previous salary alone.

Objective: Your objective in dealing with this issue is to avoid giving any answer at all. If that's not possible, your backup position is to name a range only.

Tactics:

- If you are asked this question on an application form, leave it blank.

- If you are asked in a phone interview, decline to answer by saying something like this: *"My previous salary included several factors such as base compensation and fringe benefits. When your company invites me in for an in-person interview, I will be glad to provide details."*

- If you are asked this in an interview, provide a broad range. *"My base compensation was in the 80's and there were benefits in addition."*

- Then try to establish that you want to be compensated on the basis of the job for which you are applying: *"However, I would like to add that I realize that every job is different. I am hoping we will base compensation for this job on the contribution that I will be making to your organization."*

- Finally, if you believe they are concerned that they can't afford you based on your previous compensation, you may want to say something like this: *"I was well compensated in my previous position, but my primary concern is to find a great fit with a company that will use my abilities and allow me to grow with them."*

Danger Zone #2: You may be asked, "What do you need to earn in order to take this job?"

Of course, this is a variation on "what did you make previously?" The dangers are similar but there are slight variations in your tactics.

Objective: Again, your objective is to avoid giving any answer at all. If that's not possible, your backup position is to name a range only.

Tactics:

- If you are asked, "How much do you need to earn here", give a response like this: *I'm sure you probably have a range in mind that you work with. In light of my experiences, skills and qualifications, I would like to think that I would fall near the top of your range. If you don't mind me asking, what is the normal range for this position?"*

Sure, the interviewer may push you for a specific number. Continue to hedge by stating a number for your base compensation but add that it does not include the value of the very generous benefits package your previous position provided.

Remember, the first person to name a number loses!

Asking for the Job

Any sales professional will tell you that it's important to close the sale and ask for the business. The same thing applies to job interviewing! During the conclusion of the interview, possibly when you are asked if you have any questions, as discussed below, you may want to ask for the job. I am assuming that you have collected enough information and insight by this point to determine that you actually want the job. Some ways of asking include:

- *When can I start?*
- *Is there any additional information you need from me in order to make an offer?*
- *I am interested in this job. Are we able to come to an agreement today?*

Do You Have Any Questions for Me? Why, Yes, I Do!

At the end of most interviews, you will likely be asked by the interviewer, "Do you have any other questions for me?" You should have several questions covering three topics:

1. Questions about the firm's direction and how your job will support the strategy

2. Questions about the job itself

3. Questions about your status as a candidate and how to follow-up

Here are some typical questions:

- What are the future goals of the company?

- Should you hire me for the position, how will I be supporting these future goals?
- What are your primary expectations for the person who fills this position?
- How will I know that I have met your goals?
- Why is this position vacant?
- Do you promote from within?
- Do you have a formal training program?
- How would you describe your company's corporate culture?
- How will my performance be evaluated, and how often?
- How does your selection process work?
- How many other candidates are you interviewing?
- How qualified am I in comparison with the other candidates?
- Will I be hearing from you or should I contact you?

You should also ask for the job! If you have heard enough to decide that you want the job, ask for it. Say something like this:

- *When will I be able to begin?*
- *Will we be able to come to an agreement today?*
- *I am very interested in this job. Should I be expecting an offer?*

Interview Follow-up

The one question that will save you some trouble later: *When may I contact you to follow up?*

Hiring processes can be very slow. If you don't ask the follow-up question, after a week to 10 days of waiting, you will be pacing the floor, wondering if it's OK to call or e-mail someone. So go ahead and get some guidance on how to follow up while you are there.

Regardless of the answer, immediately following the interview, send a personally written thank-you card to each interviewer. It is always appropriate to thank people for their time even if you believe the interview went poorly.

Can you use e-mail? These days, you probably can get by with it. However, should you use e-mail? Probably not. A thank-you card is a much classier!

12

Negotiate Like a Pro

My brother is a very successful civil engineer. However, at age 49, he realized future advancement in his firm likely was limited.

When an opportunity presented itself to interview with another engineering firm for a job with the scope of responsibilities he really wanted, he weighed the risks and decided to go for the interview.

Afterward, we talked about his next steps and I decided to send him an email containing a few thoughts about negotiating his compensation package. Here is his reply:

> Bud:
>
> That first item is a winner and one that I was falling prey to. One of the reasons I even considered the interview was because I feel undervalued where I am, yet I WAS using my current benefits as the starting point. No longer!

My brother, a skilled engineer as well as a savvy people person (and yes, I know, you don't always find those two skill sets combined in one person) avoided a classic error in negotiating an external upward move – the error that I described in my email to him. Here is what I had said:

> I know you are going to get a great offer and will work through it skillfully but it's just my nature to offer the information I have. So here are a few extra thoughts:
>
> Don't negotiate on the basis of your current position or compensation package; do your homework and negotiate on the basis of
>
> - The scope and scale of the position you will be taking

- The market value of the position you will be taking
- The value to the company of goals you will be achieving

In the end my brother interviewed, negotiated, received and accepted an excellent offer and made the transition. So remember, if you are attempting the difficult maneuver of an external upward move, there are pre-requisites to negotiation success. In fact, the four points below apply to negotiating for any position:

#1. Do your homework. Research until you are confident that you know the market value of the new position. Know what leading competitors of the hiring firm pay for similar positions. Know the industry standard compensation for the position.

#2. Clarify the value of the role to the hiring firm. What is it that the firm will expect you to achieve? How do those achievements relate to the firms plans and strategic imperatives? What is the value to the firm of those achievements?

#3. Clarify the scope and scale of the responsibilities. Ensure the hiring firm (i.e., your interviewer) articulates the level of responsibility you will be carrying. Understand to whom you will report, what level of decision-making responsibility you will have and how much latitude you will be granted.

#4. Control the conversation. Steer talk of compensation toward the idea of the market-value of the position, the scope and scale of responsibilities and the value of the achievements.

For example, consider the common conundrum that is addressed earlier in this book, responding to the question, "What is your current compensation?" This is an appropriate time to take control of the conversation with a comment like this one:

"My current base salary is in the $90,000 – $99,000 range. I feel

that is a somewhat below par level of compensation for my current position. However, I am surprised you are asking because I thought that we were talking about a position that is larger in scope than what I currently do."

Depending on the interviewer's response, you may have an opportunity to expand the idea a little further.

Suppose, for another example, the interviewer says, "By the way, what were you thinking of as an appropriate level of compensation?"

You don't have to respond in a heavy-handed way at all, nor do you want to back yourself into a corner. Still, you can say something like this:

"Well, I am sure that you will make a great offer. I understand that positions of this type in our industry typically pay between $125k and $175k. Is that the general range that you are considering?"

You will have made your point that "positions of this type" is the appropriate basis of compensation negotiation, not your previous package.

The Four Components of Compensation

There's a negotiating axiom about negotiating a financed purchase which states you trade off price and terms. In other words, you can pay a higher price in exchange for a lower interest rate on the financed portion. Or if you offer a lower price, the seller may accept if you agree to pay a higher interest rate on the financed portion. You negotiate between price and terms.

A similar concept can help you in negotiating compensation for a job: salary and benefits. You may be able to accept a lower base salary if the benefits package can be sweetened or vice versa.

There are four major components of compensation and you should have a mental list of all of them! A simple tactic is to ask about each of the following items at some point during the negotiation and interviewing phases.

Compensation Component #1: Transition Arrangements

- A sign-on bonus (perhaps the benefit that job candidates most often fail to ask about)
- Relocation compensation

Compensation Component #2: Salary

- Base pay
- Sales commissions

Compensation Component #3: Benefits

- Adequate budget
- Annual bonuses
- Child care subsidy
- Company car and car allowance
- Conference costs and expenses
- Deferred compensation
- Frequency of performance reviews
- Frequency of salary reviews
- Incentives and profit sharing
- Insurance - life, medical, dental, disability
- Reporting relationships
- Retirement plans and contributions
- Scope of responsibility
- Tele-work, tele-commuting
- Training and development
- Travel (for yourself and your spouse)
- Tuition reimbursement
- Vacation, sick days, sabbaticals, leaves

Remember, you can negotiate for the provision of these benefits *or* the enhancement of these benefits. For example:

> *"Yes, I could possibly accept the salary you have suggested although it is a little under what I was hoping. However, I notice that you normally start people with one week of vacation. In light of the lower salary, I would feel better about accepting the offer if you could start me at two weeks of vacation annually. What would it take to make that possible?"*

Compensation Component #4: Exit Compensation

Executives get golden parachutes. You don't have to go that far but there are often negotiable exit compensation issues.

- Severance pay
- Outplacement services

General Principles of Good Negotiating

1st – Know what a win is.

Never enter negotiations before you have determined your personal top and bottom numbers. You should know the absolute *least* compensation you must have, regardless of how much you want a particular job. That's your *bottom* number.

You should also determine the absolute *highest* compensation you believe you can command. That's your *top* number. Any compensation you negotiate that falls between the two is a win!

2nd – Know what fair is.

Do your homework! Research the normal salary range for a person with your experience in the job and industry, with consideration of the part of the country you are in and the size of the firm. You can find a lot of information on websites such as Salary.com.

However, this is also a great way to use your personal network. Ask around and talk to anyone who knows the company. Better yet, find a contact inside the company. Do your industrial espionage and find out as much as you can about what the company pays. At a minimum, arrive at an estimated range of a fair salary.

3rd – Do *not* back yourself into a corner.

Even though you *know* your bottom number, never state it. If at all possible, avoid stating a flat number for your salary expectation. Always use a range. If the interviewer offers the information, "Our salary for this position is $x", even if the number is below your bottom number, don't just end the interview. The point is to always keep a flexible frame of mind. Take the attitude that anything can be negotiated and you will fare well. If you complete an interview process and never are able to arrive at a satisfactory conclusion, no harm done! At least you tried.

4th – Wait.

Do *not* bring up compensation until the employer makes you an offer. I have previously discussed ways to avoid providing flat numbers about your desired level of compensation.

You are in a much more powerful negotiating position if you delay discussions of compensation until *after* the firm has decided they want you! Do everything you can to put off discussion until then.

5th – Think it over.

You don't need to accept or reject immediately. It sometimes happens that simply saying "I need to think it over for a day" will result in an increase in the original offer. I have never heard of an employer demanding that a candidate decide on the spot. Most will respond favorably if you ask for 24 hours to think it over.

6th – If you are disappointed with *the offer*, show it but be careful to also show excitement for *the job*.

If the offer is significantly less than you expected or wanted or even if it is out of your "win" range, you don't have to say "no" on the spot. Try this: simply look down at the floor and be quiet for a long pause. Count to 10. Hopefully, the person making the offer will ask, "What's wrong?"

You reply, "I am really interested in this job. However, I have to admit, the offer is significantly less than I expected." Then stop talking and wait.

This tactic very well may bring an immediate discussion of what it would take to be more acceptable. However, even if this tactic does not bring any movement from the person making the offer, nothing is lost. You didn't say you didn't want the job. You indicated that you are interested. You can follow up by using the suggestion made previously, "Make I take 24 hours to consider your offer?"

Take the 24 hours and think it over. If it is below your lowest win number, decline the offer. If it is high enough to be a win, even though it may not be fair, you may decide to accept the offer.

Good luck with your negotiations. The easiest money you will ever make is the concessions you arrange from a new employer when you negotiate your compensation!

Necessity never made a good bargain.

~Benjamin Franklin~

Think Outside the Cubicle

"Losing my job was the best thing that ever happened to me," said Larry. "It gave me the chance to make changes in my career that I had been thinking about a long time."

Larry isn't alone. Many people use career transitions to launch new careers, even new lifestyles. Career transition can be the perfect time to reach deep and resurrect old dreams of moving to a different part of the country, going back to school or starting a business.

If you are in career transition, maybe it's time to think outside the cubicle! This chapter provides some creative possibilities for you to consider.

Consider Relocating - Go West, Young Man

Forbes.com reports, "In hard times, metropolitan areas in Texas and college towns hold out the best opportunities for employment."ˣ Here's another clue: the top five are all in Texas!

The article lists the 10 best large cities for jobs in America. Selection is based on job growth in regions across the U.S. over the long, middle and short term. The authors admit that economic growth recently has been very poor everywhere and the current list may reflect the "least worst" areas of growth. Still, fact is, some areas of the country are better for jobs than others. Here's the Forbes' list for 2009:

> 10. Portland – Vancouver – Beaverton, Washington, Oregon
> 9. Oklahoma City, Oklahoma
> 8. Raleigh – Cary, North Carolina
> 7. Salt Lake City, Utah

6. Seattle – Bellevue – Everett, Washington
5. Dallas – Plano – Irving, Texas
4. Fort Worth – Arlington, Texas
3. San Antonio, Texas
2. Houston – Sugar Land – Baytown, Texas
1. Austin – Round Rock, Texas

Consider Going Back to School - The Route to 3 Million Jobs

A 2009 edition of **Business Week** states:

> "Surprising statistic: In the midst of the worst recession in a generation or more, with 13 million people unemployed, there are approximately 3 million jobs that employers are actively recruiting for but so far have been unable to fill. That's more job openings than the entire population of Mississippi."

Sound like good news? It's not. Instead, it's evidence of an emerging structural shift in the U.S. economy that has created serious mismatches between workers and employers.

People thrown out of shrinking sectors such as construction, finance and retail lack the skills and training for openings in growing fields including education, accounting, health care, and government. At the same time, the worst housing bust in decades has left the unemployed frozen in place. They can't move to get work because they can't sell their homes.

So what does this mean for you?

First, consider retraining. Secondly, unfortunately, the best opportunity for a new job may be a move downward.

While rules and programs vary from state to state, there are funds available at state unemployment offices, one stop centers and workforce development   centers for   retraining   of   displaced workers. This could be your route to one of 3 million available jobs!

Entrepreneurship

Millions are currently unemployed. The job market is flooded with qualified candidates. Businesses across the country have frozen hiring. It's tough to get a job without a protracted search.

Many who lost their jobs are considering starting a business. You may be one of them. Perhaps you've had a business idea in the back of your mind for a long time. Maybe you just don't think you will find a job again. Either way, it may seem that circumstances have conspired to give you a push in the direction of business ownership.

Entrepreneurship is not for everyone, but it may be for you! The first thing to do is to take a personal inventory.

Are You the Entrepreneurial Type?

There are plenty of entrepreneurial personality tests online. It may be worth your while to take a couple of them, review the results, and give them due consideration. I wouldn't take any of them as gospel but they will raise important issues for you to consider, such as your tolerance for risk.

If you don't want to go to the trouble to do that, at least consider the following article from SCORE, an organization of retired business executives and owners who volunteer their time consulting with entrepreneurs.

Do You Have the Mindset and Skills to be an Entrepreneur?

You probably already know that starting a small business requires extensive research and analysis of many factors.

But the one requiring the most critical assessment is often overlooked by many entrepreneurs. And, it's as close as the nearest mirror.

That's because *wanting* to be an entrepreneur is one thing; *being* one is quite another. You will take on responsibilities and commitments far different from those of an employee, even if you have management experience. It's a challenge that can be exhilarating and rewarding. Unless you're prepared mentally and emotionally, however, it can also be overwhelming.

Before you study financing options and plan store layouts, sit down and conduct a probing interview with yourself to see if you're the right person for the all-important job of entrepreneur-owner-boss.

Are You a Self-Starter?
Nothing in business happens by itself. As the owner, you're responsible for everything from establishing your firm's vision to setting the daily work schedule. The fact that you're exploring small business ownership and asking questions is a good sign.

Are You a Positive Thinker?
The moment you become a business owner, you represent yourself, your business and your expectations for success. What you say and do must convey confidence and commitment to moving forward. Employees who sense these qualities will share that determination to succeed, even under difficult circumstances. If you work alone … you have to be your own cheerleader.

Are You Disciplined?
Your days of the "9-to-5 routine" are over. Running a small business requires a continuous commitment to quality and detail. You cannot afford to cut corners, miss

deadlines or make promises beyond your capabilities. If you plan to run the business from home, you must be able to resist temptations and distractions in order to get your work done.

Are You a Lifelong Learner?

Entrepreneurs who continually seek information, new ideas and sound advice have the best chance for success. Being attuned to market trends and issues makes it easier to adjust products and services to customers' needs and preferences. You're also in a better position to enhance your competitive advantage and efficiency, and address potential problems before they harm your business.

Can You Market Yourself and Your Business?

Some people have trouble with this one because of the negative (and often unfair) connotations associated with being a "salesperson." No business, no matter how good, will succeed without some kind of marketing. The good news is that promoting your business is easier than you may think as long as you know what to do and how to do it. After all, we all enjoy saying good things about ourselves. When you craft and tell your story in the right way, more people will be willing and eager to hear it.

Can You be Objective?

Your ideas and practices may seem "bulletproof," but reality may be far different. Is there really a need for a particular product or service in your area? Are the hours of operation fair to your employees? Is renting equipment better than owning it? A good business owner knows how to examine an issue from many perspectives and understand that strengths and limitations of each.

So how did your "candidate" for entrepreneur-owner-boss do? If every answer was a "yes," your small business dream is on its way to becoming a reality. For areas of concern, the solution may be business counseling, management courses, or a concerted effort to discard some unproductive habits in favor new ones.

Finally, make it a point to conduct regular self-reviews. Thinking and approaches that worked in the start-up phase may not be as appropriate for a thriving concern, or if a major market shift occurs. When you work for yourself, you want to be confident the entrepreneur-owner-boss knows exactly what he or she is doing.[xi]

Take the First Steps

Still think you have the right stuff? In that case, get started! Here are three things you must have to get started.

1. **The idea.** You may already have an idea in mind. If not, start brainstorming. A great idea will probably intersect your passion, your experience, and a solution for a specific target market. You will need to decide if you prefer to start a business from scratch, buy an existing business, or purchase a franchise.

2. **The plan.** Don't think you can succeed with a great idea only. You need a plan supported by real market research. There are plenty of books and on-line resources to tell you how to go about creating a business plan.

3. **The license.** Actually, your city, county and state governments may require several business licenses and permits. You may also need licenses and permits required by the federal government. Requirements vary so check with all levels of government.

Additional Resources for Entrepreneurs

Here are additional resources to help you evaluate and start your entrepreneurial enterprise.

Books and Magazines:

The E-Myth (available at bookstores) by Michael E. Gerber

Entrepreneur Magazine www.entrepreneur.com

Organizations:

Association of Small Business Development Centers www.asbdc-us.org/

SCORE www.score.org

Small Business Administration www.sba.gov

Contract Labor

Many companies cut too deeply during recessions and find themselves without key human resources they need to perform vital functions. So they hire back the same people they fired, only this time as contract labor. In fact, as economies recover, growth in the contracting market may precede growth in the labor market.

Bottom line is that you may find work on a contractual basis much faster than you will as a hired-on employee. Frankly, this is especially true for those over the age of 50. Contracting may not be a bad deal for you if you are of an entrepreneurial bent, very independent or only want some income and don't need health insurance or other benefits.

You should familiarize yourself with applicable laws and like any entrepreneur you must have some ability to market yourself.

You can find out more at Score.com.

Encore Careers

Encore.org provides information about encore careers – second careers following retirement that focus on personal fulfillment and social change.

According to the website Encore.org:

> "Encore.org is published by Civic Ventures, a nonprofit think tank that is leading the call to engage millions of experienced individuals in becoming a force for social change. Civic Ventures focuses on creating pathways to encore careers that provide continued income doing work that is personally fulfilling and helps address some of society's biggest challenges."[xii]

Perhaps the loss of your job is an opportunity to take a whole new direction in life in a career that focuses on serving others.

So You Want To Work At Home

Do you want to work at home?

Many people do and many infomercials and websites promise you can! Afraid that some of those claims may be exaggerated? You're smart to think that because many of them are just what you fear – rip-offs.

However, there are legitimate work-at-home opportunities and there are two ways to go: either look at a work from home opportunity that is advertised as such, or seek out companies that may have work from home policies.

First, learn what to avoid. The Better Business Bureau offers a good article detailing the six most common scams.

Most Common Scams

To protect yourself, learn to recognize the most common work-at-home scams.

ASSEMBLY WORK AT-HOME: <u>Typical Ad</u> -- "Assembly work at home! Easy money assembling craft items. No experience necessary."

This scheme requires you to invest hundreds of dollars in instructions and materials and many hours of your time to produce items such as baby booties, toy clowns, and plastic signs for a company that has promised to buy them. Once you have purchased the supplies and have done the work, the company often decides not to pay you because your work does not meet certain "standards." You are then left with merchandise that is difficult or impossible to sell.

CHAIN LETTER: <u>Typical Ad</u> -- "Make copies of this letter and send them to people whose names we will provide. All you have to do is send us ten dollars for our mailing list and labels. Look at the chart below and see how you will automatically receive thousands in cash return!!!"

The only people who benefit from chain letters are the mysterious few at the top of the chain who constantly change names, addresses, and post office boxes. They may attempt to intimidate you by threatening bad luck, or try to impress you by describing themselves as successful professionals who know all about non-existent sections of alleged legal codes.

ENVELOPE STUFFING: Typical Ad -- "$350 Weekly Guaranteed! Work two hours daily at home stuffing envelopes."

When answering such ads, you may not receive the expected envelopes for stuffing, but instead get promotional material asking for cash just for details on money-making plans. The details usually turn out to be instructions on how to go into the business of placing the same kind of ad the advertiser ran in the first place. Pursuing the envelope ad plan may require spending several hundred dollars more for advertising, postage, envelopes, and printing. This system feeds on continuous recruitment of people to offer the same plan. There are several variations on this type of scheme, all of which require the customer to spend money on advertising and materials. According to the U.S. Postal Inspection Service, "In practically all businesses, envelope stuffing has become a highly mechanized operation using sophisticated mass mailing techniques and equipment which eliminates any profit potential for an individual doing this type of work-at-home. The Inspection Service knows of no work-at-home promotion that ever produces income as alleged."

MULTI-LEVEL MARKETING: Typical Ad -- "Our products make it possible for people like you to earn more than they ever have in their lives! Soon you can let others earn money for you while you and your family relax and enjoy your affluent lifestyle! No experience necessary."

Multi-level marketing, a direct sales system, is a well-established, legitimate form of business. Many people have successfully sold the products of reputable companies to their neighbors and co-workers.

These people are independent distributors who sell popular products and also recruit other distributors to join them. On the other hand, illegitimate pyramid schemes can resemble these legitimate direct sales systems. An obvious difference is that the emphasis is on recruiting others to join the program, not on selling the product. For a time, new recruits who make the investment to buy product samples keep money coming into the system, but very few products are sold. Sooner or later the people on the bottom are stuck with a saturated market, and they cannot make money by selling products or recruiting. When the whole system collapses, only a few people at the top have made money—and those at the bottom have lost their investment.

ONLINE BUSINESS: <u>Typical Ad</u> -- "Turn your Home Computer into a Cash Machine! Get computer diskette FREE! Huge Selection of Jobs! No experience needed! Start earning money in days! Many companies want to expand, but don't want to pay for office space. You save them money by working in the comfort of your home."

This is typical of advertisements showing up uninvited in your e-mail—an old scheme advertised in a new way. You pay for a useless guide to work-at-home jobs—a mixture of computer-related work such as word processing or data entry and the same old envelope-stuffing and home crafts scams.

The computer disk is as worthless as the guidebook. It may only list free government web sites and/or business opportunities which require more money.

PROCESSING MEDICAL INSURANCE CLAIMS: <u>Typical Ad</u> -- "You can earn from $800 to $1000 weekly processing insurance claims on your home computer for health care professionals such as doctors, dentists chiropractors, and podiatrists. Over 80% of providers need your services. Learn how in one day!"

Generally, the promoter of this scheme attracts you by advertising on cable television and, perhaps, by inviting you to a business opportunity trade show at a hotel or convention center. You may be:

- Urged to buy software programs and even computers at exorbitant prices; a program selling at a software store for $69 might cost you several thousands of dollars.
- Told that your work will be coordinated with insurance companies by a central computer.
- Required to pay for expensive training sessions available at a "current special rate" that will be higher in the future, and
- Pressured to make a decision immediately.

Most likely, the expensive training sessions are superficial, and the market for your services is very small or nonexistent. The promoter may delay the processing of your job, citing a backlog or mistakes in your work. There may also be no central computer as advertised. You may be left with no way to deliver what you have promised to your clients or customers—if you found any—and with no way to earn any money on you own.[xiii]

The Federal Trade Commission has similar concerns. However, there are legitimate work-at-home opportunities.

First, there are many traditional brick and mortar companies that offer tele-commuting opportunities. Use your network, ask around and you may find some companies that will allow you to work out of your home.

In addition, there are legitimate "virtual" organizations that use the work at home model. Most are going to offer some kind of customer service position and pay is going to work out to $10 - $12 hourly. However, in many cases, your schedule can be completely flexible. A good source of information is the Work at Home Moms website (don't let the name of the website fool you – their information applies to anyone working from home). Find them at www.wahm.com.

Here are websites of a few reputable work-at-home employers:

www.alpineaccess.com

www.liveops.com

www.gowillow.com

www.workingsol.com

Federal Government Jobs

Here's the scoop: a lot of people want federal government jobs. They're not easy to get. However, if you are persistent, it can be done. The obstacles include a complex and difficult hiring process which includes special requirements for résumés.

Locating Federal Government Jobs

Every government agency has its own website and some (such as the C.I.A.) have their own application process.

However, www.usajobs.gov is the official job site of the US Federal Government and states that it is your one-stop source for Federal jobs and employment information. The U.S. Postal Service is one exception, however.

Consider Temporary and Contract Federal Jobs

You may want to consider applying for temporary and contract Federal jobs. They can segue into permanent federal jobs and generate experience and contacts that may lead to permanent jobs. Besides, the temporary agencies or contractors may hire faster than federal agencies do.

Identify federal contract jobs using the websites of federal contractors. A list of the nation's top 100 contractors is posted at www.usaspending.gov.   Identify temporary agencies that serve federal agencies staff at www.state.gov/m/dghr/flo/c21666.htm.

Federal Government Résumé and Cover Letter Requirements

Most government applications are done through online résumé builders.   Cover letters generally are not necessary or needed but additional documents are often required. A prime example is a Key Skills Area (KSA) summary addressing the candidate's qualification/experience in each of the KSA areas outlined for that particular position. Job postings should contain complete application instructions. *It is essential to understand that **all required information must be provided** or your entire application will be ignored!*

Conclusion:
You Can Do This!

One last word: you can do this!

Loss of a job and career transition is one of the most stressful events you will ever face. Job loss affects your sense of identity. It challenges self-esteem.

Then, while reeling under those pressures, you have to start facing the inherent potential for rejection that goes with any job search.

The job seeker faces a very big challenge at a very weak moment. Throw a bad economy into the mix and you have the recipe for discouragement, anxiety and maybe even depression.

You will need to reach into your spiritual resources to draw the strength you need. Dig deep into your faith, reach out to your family and friends, pray for help and stay in motion!

At the deepest, darkest moments of the recession during early 2009, if you had listened to the news, you would have literally thought no one in America was getting a job. However, I saw people even during that bleak period landing good jobs every week.

When I first started as a career consultant, I thought my work with a client was done when the client landed a job. In retrospect, that's a paternalistic attitude.

Not too long into this line of work, I spoke with one of my first clients. He had not landed a job. However, we had come a long way in helping him understand many of the kinds of topics that are in this book. More importantly, as his level of knowledge increased, so did his self-confidence.

One day he made a statement to me the totally reframed the way I understand my career consulting work.

> *"Bud, I now have the tools, the plan and the attitude I need to conduct my own job search. I will find a job!"*

He did find a job!

You will, too; not only "a job" but a good job, even in a bad economy.

You can do this!

Appendices

Hablas El Espanol?

Spanish speaking job search links:

www.latpro.com

www.ihispano.com

www.hispanic-jobs.com

There are some job boards that have a feature allowing you to change them into other languages.

Got a Record? Concerned About Background Checks?

Most major contracting/staffing firms require background checks for all candidates.

Many client companies will tell their staffing firm they don't want to interview anyone with a felony background. Your best bet in some cases may be to work with the state unemployment office. They may be aware of employers willing to work with you.

The most important challenge you may face is discouragement and rebuilding your self-confidence. Work hard on staying positive!

Résumé Worksheet

This is the information you will need to gather before writing your résumé.

General Information

Current address

Phone number(s) and e-mail(s) where you can be contacted

Your highest level of education

Name of school

City and state of school

If you graduated, certificate or degree and date of graduation

If did not graduate, the major or name of the course work

Additional training, certifications and/or degrees

Name of the training, certificate or degree

Name of the institutions or companies that provided the training, certificate or degree

Date the training, certificate or degree was completed or granted

List of community associations or any volunteer work that would be directly relevant to the type job you are seeking

Job History (for the last 10 years)

Gather the information below for each job title you have held during the last 10 years.

Company name

Company location - city and state

Dates of employment at the company

Job title

Dates of employment in that position

Main job responsibilities

Accomplishments and awards

Tools, equipment, certifications, licences or software used on this job

Endnotes

[i] Retrieved from
http://www.mint.com/blog/finance-core/a-visual-guide-to-the-
financial-crisis-unemployment-rates/
on June 10, 2009.

[ii] Retrieved from
http://msn.careerbuilder.com/Article/MSN-1208-Job-Search-
Rebound-from-
Rejection/?sc_extcmp=JS_1208_advice&SiteId=cbmsn41208
on June 11, 2009

[iii] Retrieved from
http://online.wsj.com/article/SB100014240529702038724045742
60032327828514.html
on September 9, 2009

[iv] Retrieved from
http://www.rocket-hire.com/_pdf/2007/2007-Recruiting-
Trends-Whitepaper.pdf
on September 9, 2009

[v] Retrieved from http://www.bersin.com/Blog/post/7-
Elevene28099s-New-and-Improved-Sourcing-Strategy-Will-
Social-Media-Replace-Job-Boards.aspx
on September 9, 2009

[vi] Name changed; all other details are unaltered.

[vii] Retrieved from
http://hotjobs.yahoo.com/career-experts-
10_boilerplate_phrases_that_kill_resumes-97
on October 16, 2009

[viii] Current as of June 2009

[ix] Retrieved from
http://online.wsj.com/article/SB124390348922474789.html
on October 21, 2009

[x] Retrieved from http://www.forbes.com/2009/04/14/best-cities-for-jobs-opinions-columnists-employment.html
on October 28, 2009

[xi] Retrieved from
http://www.score.org/mindset_skills_entrepreneur.html
on October 23, 2009

[xii] Retrieved from
http://www.encore.org/about
on October 28, 2009

[xiii] Retrieved on
http://www.bbb.org/us/article/408
on October 28, 2009

How To Order This Book

Order on-line at
www.amazon.com

Contact Bud Clarkson

I wrote this book to help the millions who are unemployed, under-employed or simply hate their jobs.

Feel free to contact me personally with questions or comments.

Bud Clarkson
(419) 517-6151

Bud@JobSearchStrategiesBook.com

Visit
www.JobSearchStrategiesBook.com

www.ingramcontent.com/pod-product-compliance
Lightning Source LLC
Chambersburg PA
CBHW051521170526
45165CB00002B/557